The _New_ Forms Kit for Early Childhood Programs

Director-Approved and Ready-to-Use Forms for Every Need

Early Childhood Directors Association

Redleaf Press

A division of Resources for Child Caring

© 1992 Early Childhood Directorss Association

All Rights Reserved

ISBN: 0-934140-76-6

Published by: Redleaf Press
                     Formerly Toys 'n Things Press
                     a division of Resources for Child Caring
                     450 North Syndicate, Suite 5
                     St. Paul, Minnesota   55104

Distributed by: Gryphon House
                     P.O. Box   275
                     Mt. Rainier, Maryland 20712

Library of Congress Cataloging-in-Publication Data

The New forms kit for early childhood program : director-approved and
  ready-to-use forms for every need / Early Childhood Directors
  Association.
      p.   cm.
   ISBN 0-934140-76-6 : $24.95
   1. Early childhood education — United States— Forms. 2. School
records — United States.   I. Early Childhood Directors Association.
LB1139.25.N49 1992
372.21— dc20   92-32447
                                                   CIP

Printed in the United States of America

The Early Childhood Directors Association ECDA wants to help you streamline your administrative tasks. Fifty-one directors have combined their experience and expertise to create this publication.

This book contains over 165 new forms that were not published in our previous edition, FORMS KIT FOR DIRECTORS. The publication committee received many high quality samples of forms from ECDA members, and then combined the new and updated forms with the best forms in our first book.

As with POLICIES AND PROCEDURES FOR EARLY CHILDHOOD DIRECTORS, this publication is designed so you can reproduce the forms for your program. We strongly believe that there is no reason to " re-invent the wheel," so you may modify any of these forms to meet the specific needs of your program.

This publication is designed for use in child care centers, nursery schools, and other early childhood programs. The publication committee hopes that you enjoy this book, and that it helps make your job a little easier.

About the Early Childhood Directors Association

ECDA is a statewide professional organization serving two hundred and seventy-five directors throughout the state of Minnesota as well as some out-of-state members. Our association is recognized both locally and nationally for publishing materials designed specifically for early childhood professionals.

ECDA received its non-profit corporate status in 1979, and writing publications such as this one is one of our main focuses. In 1983, we began writing books that would be published on a national basis, and every year we have produced another publication to enhance the professionalism of this field. The members of ECDA want to share their knowledge so others may save hours of administrative time.

043369

Acknowledgements

Although this book represents the work of many individuals who developed the forms, a core group of individuals spent many hours soliciting forms, selecting forms to be used and organizing the book itself. These individuals are:

Alice Marks

Barbara Matthews

Karen Fischer

Lynn Jessen

Mary Szlaius

Tina Liiste

Special recognition is accorded three people whose special efforts made this book happen.

Barbara Wigstadt

Linda Reusch

Susan Wick

This book would have been impossible to complete without their commitment and dedication. THANKS!

Contributors

These forms are those developed by directors for their own use, or passed down through centers from one director to another. It was not always possible to determine the original source. They represent and may include formats developed from the collective wisdom of many people, conferences, workshops and classes held on a local, state, or national level.

We are grateful to those early childhood professionals who unknowingly contributed through their teaching to this book, and therefore are not listed below.

Adventure Club

Baby Care

Bloomington Child Development Association

Bright Start Children's Center

Calvary Child Care Center

Capitol Child Care

Carol Mathey's Memorial Center

Children's Country Day School

Children's Home Society of Minnesota

Civic League Day Nursery

Close to Home

Community Day Care Association

Country Way Preschool

Creative Play Learning Center

Cricket Child Care Center

Downtown Day Care Center

First Trinity Creative Child Care

Friendship Day Care Center

Golden Heart Child Care Center

Home-In-Stead Day Care

Jack and Jill Nursery School

Just for Kids

Kids R Special

Kids Time, Inc.

Mercy Child Care

Messiah Preschool

Model Cities Child Care

North Como Preschool

Paidea Child Development Center

Presentation Childhood Learning Center

Rainbow School

Roseville Lutheran Nursery School

Salem Community Child Care

Sandcastle Child Care

South Park Day Care

Southside Family Nurturing Center

State of Minnesota - Department of Human Services

St. Catherine's Early Childhood Center

St. Croix Day Care Center

St. Mary's Day Care

St. Matthew's Child Care

St. Paul's Childhood Center

St. Paul's Episcopal Preschool

St. Paul Public Schools

St. Timothy's Parent Participation Preschool

Sunshine Child Care Center

Susan Wick Consulting

The L & N School

TLC Day Care

Warm World Child Development Center

Woodview Terrace Montessori

Table of Contents

Table of Contents

Table of Contents

© Early Childhood Directors Association (ECDA) 450 North Syndicate, Suite 5, St. Paul, MN 55104

Table of Contents

Marketing and Long–Range Planning

Marketing
In this section you will find forms to guide you through the process of developing your marketing plan, implementing your ideas, creating new ideas and evaluating your efforts.

Long Range Planning
In this section you will find forms to either get you started or refresh your skills in long range planning. This section could be used as a complete resource for start to finish long range planning or each form can be used on its own as needed.

Defining Your Market

1. Who is your market?_____

    A. What ages of children do you wish to serve?_____

    B. What area of the community do you wish to serve?_____

    C. What socioeconomic community will you serve?_____

    D. What family constellation will you appeal to?_____

2. What needs are you meeting?_____

    A. Full day care?_____

    B. Nursery school programming?_____

    C. Requirement for number of days of attendance?_____

    D. Is drop in care provided?_____

    E. Evening care/sick care/etc?_____

    F. Flexible care?_____

Once you have answered these questions, you will be in a position to write a definition of your marketing plan.

Determining Your Sales Potential (to evaluate yearly)

1. Evaluate your current potential customer marketplace.

    A. Population of families with children_____

    B. Demographics of children in your service age range_____

    C. Median income of families with young children_____

    D. Occupation of parents
    (Example: professional, semiprofessional, industrial, mixed, students, etc.)_____

2. Evaluate the current competition.

    A. How many centers are providing similar service in a five mile area from your center?_____

    B. How many expansions of current programs and/or changes have been experienced by these programs in the past five years?

    _____

    C. Contact your city/county planning and zoning commission for any plans for new programs in your area.

Community Awareness

1. What are the licensing requirements?_____

_____

2. Are there any new or proposed changes in licensing, zoning or health?_____

_____

3. What are the needs being felt by the business community? Contact your Chamber of Commerce and personnel departments of corporations.

_____

_____

4. What are the needs being felt by the government? Contact city, county and state offices.

_____

_____

5. Contact local builders and realtors to find out how they perceive the demographics of the community.

Chart & Analyze Data From Past Records & Current Inquiries

1. Which groups have the highest attendance; note time of year or set patterns in data.

_____

_____

2. When parents request information, what service hours do they need?_____

_____

3. What age groups are they currently requesting?_____

_____

4 What other services are they looking for?_____

_____

5. How many families did not enroll, why?_____

_____

6. Why did they call or visit your program?_____

_____

Attracting Customers

1. What is your image-how the community identifies you? (Very Important!)_____

_____

2. How does your price compare with other programs in your area?_____

_____

3. Do your customer service policies represent services needed by the families in your area?_____

_____

4. Have you investigated advertising in the phases of media that will most likely reach your designated market?

_____

_____

- -

Attracting Customers

1. What is your image-how the community identifies you. (Very Important!)_____

_____

2. How does your price compare with other programs in your area?_____

_____

3. Do your customer service policies represent services needed by the families in your area?_____

_____

4. Have you investigated advertising in the phases of media that will most likely reach your designated market?_____

_____

_____

Marketing Ideas

1. Referral Credit
   To parents: pick $ amount and credit toward child care when people referred have been in attendance one month

   To staff: direct cash payment to staff person referring or credit toward child care, if they have children in your program and care is not a benefit

2. Quality curriculum and sell curriculum.
   - "sell" individual attention
   - "sell" philosophy
   - "sell" "discovery" areas
   - "sell" staff—stress most positive qualities and how well they work together. Find out what the parent thinks is important and highlight how your program meets their need. Whatever you think is great about your program, "sell" it!

3. Collaborate with local and/or area businesses using coupons for child care credit and/or merchandise as exchange.

4. Collaborate with major businesses and referral agencies.

5. Get "newcomer" lists from welcome wagon, real estate agencies, etc. Send a welcome note and invite them to see your center. If feasible offer 1-2 hours or more of free or discounted child care.

6. Once a month remain open in the evening for parents to do shopping, run errands, etc.

7. Sponsor a parent/child activity day on a Saturday morning.

8. Get involved in community activities. VOLUNTEER!!!

9. Take advantage of special events like poison prevention, fire prevention, etc. Using children's pictures (child designed/drawn) make flyer and ask local grocery stores to distribute in people's grocery bags. Include brief information on center, give number and name to call.

10. Hand out your business cards to *everyone* you meet, including relatives. Don't have business cards—get some.

11. Sponsor a special children's activity and invite local newspaper to come and take pictures. (You'll have better success of it making it in the paper if you or your staff writes an article to go with it.)

12. Get involved in area/district PTA's.

13. Send child made creations (use your imagination) to new businesses—make sure name of center is boldly attached.

14. Maintain positive interactions with current parents. The BEST advertisement is word of mouth from satisfied customers.

15. Provide a list of parent referrals (satisfied parents who have agreed to be called) for prospective new parents.

16. Offer free "trial" child care by appointment.

17. Keep staff happy and paid well for lower turnover.

Public Service Announcement

These are announcements that give the public information about something other than the existence of your program. The following titles are examples of uses of PSA's.

Use PSA's whenever you sponsor a no charge community sevice or event. This is an excellent way to let the community know your program exists. If they attend the event, you will have shown your program to many potential families.

Child Safety to Be Topic on the 8th

(sponsor parent education at your center, no charge)

Warning to Parents Using Portable Playpens

(identify your center at the end)

Parents' Child Care Concerns Addressed

(hold informational meetings at your center, no charge)

Press Release

A press release is a statement of fact about your program. It is written to interest a cable TV editor or newspaper editor to publish it. The following titles are examples of uses of the press release.

Mary Smith Joins Child Care Center Staff

(write up a short description of new staff member)

Preschoolers Pick Pumpkins on Halloween

(send article about field trip with pictures)

Child Care Center Adds Toddler Program

(write up article giving enrollment info)

Use a press release, usually with a black and white picture, if any of the following things happen:
• a new staff person is added
• a field trip is taken
• an addition or change is made in program offerings or services
• special events at center, such as "Santa Visits"
• children graduate into kindergarten

Finding Media Sources In Your Community

If you live in a large metropolitan area it is important to send public service announcements and press releases to small neighborhood newspapers as well as the large papers.

Usually the local cable TV company accepts community information. This is an excellent means of exposing your program name.

Ask parents who are currently enrolled what newspapers they read. Use the following form.

Family name_____

Child(s) name_____

Periodically we send press releases to local newspapers about our program. There are two ways that you can help us accomplish this. Please take a minute to write down (below) the names of any local newspapers that you read. Then sign at the bottom of this form acknowledging permission for us to use photos of your children involved in these special activities.

Newspaper # 1 _____

Newspaper # 2 _____

Newspaper # 3 _____

I give _____Child Care Program permission to submit pictures of my children to local newspapers for use in press releases.

_____
Parent signature   Date

_____
Parent Signature   Date

© Early Childhood Directors Association (ECDA) 450 North Syndicate, Suite 5, St. Paul, MN 55104

Telephone or Walk-in Inquiries *(Circle Which Type)*

Date_____ Employee_____

Approximate Time_____A.M. or P.M.

Place an X for each category the client asked questions about.

____Tuition Cost   ____Staff Qualifications   ____Curriculum   ____Hours of Operation

____Lunch Program   ____Tuition Aid   ____Field Trips   ____Parking   ____Discipline Policies

____Special Programs(describe) _____

____Age Groups Served (check which age(s) they need care for)

____Infant   ____Toddler   ____Preschool   ____School Age

Other Questions _____

_____

Ask how they heard about our program. Please write response.

_____

If an appointment has been made to visit fill in their name and phone number:

_____

If the visit occurred finish this form:

What about our program seemed to impress them?

_____

What concerns did they express during the visit?

_____

Did they enroll their child? _____yes _____no

If yes, what day will the child begin?_____

Child's name and age?_____

Name of employee who conducted visit._____

Checklist during Parents 1st Visit

Director: This is a list of areas that child care professionals feel parents need to be informed about when choosing child care.

Whenever possible print out the following items to help the visiting parent see the quality you offer.

• Program License

• NAEYC Accreditation

• Daily, weekly, and/or monthly schedules and curriculum

• Center goals and philosophies, this could be in the parent. handbook.

• Bulletin Boards. wall displays, etc. from a childs' view.

The active examples of quality child care are important to point out to parents whenever appropriate.

• Teachers involved with all of the children in the group

• Happy and involved children

• The following balance of activity:
     indoor/outdoor
     active/quiet
     group/individual
     intellectual/artistic

• Well built attractive equipment

• Appropriate teacher-child ratios

Marketing Questionnaire to Parents

1. How did you first hear of this program?
    a. Saw the sign in the front yard
    b. Heard about it from a friend
    c. Yellow Pages
    d. Read an ad in the newspaper: Which paper? _____
    e. Referred by a public agency
    f. Church bulletin: Which Church? _____
    g. Other _____

2. Did you receive a copy of our brochure in the mail? _____

3. Was the brochure
    a. Interesting and helpful
    b. Confusing
    c. Not informative enough
    d. Other _____

4. Did you find it helpful to visit before your child starting attending?
    a. Yes
    b. No, not really

5. Was there anything memorable - positive or negative - about your visit?
    a. Yes
    b. No

    If yes, what was it? _____

6. What was the most important thing you saw that you really liked or made you decide to send your child here?
_____
_____

7. If we could offer any type of class, activity, or service to your child at the program, what would you like it to

be? _____
_____

8. Any other comments? _____
_____

Parent's Signature (optional) _____

We appreciate your telling friends and neighbors about us when you have the opportunity.
Thank you.

Parent Exit Interview

Family Name _____ Dates in attendance _____

Child's Name _____

1. Describe two strengths of our program:

_____

_____

2. Describe two weaknesses of our program:

_____

_____

3. List two (or more) suggestions for improvements or changes:

_____

_____

4. Why are you leaving?

_____

_____

5. Would you like to be kept on our mailing list to be informed of future events at our program?

_____

_____

Parent Exit Interview

Dear Parent,

You and your child recently left _____. To help us make decisions about the child care services we provide, we are asking you to answer the following questions about the services you received at _____ and why you decided to leave.

Please return the completed questionnaire in the attached self-addressed, stamped envelope. Your cooperation will be greatly appreciated.

Sincerely, _____

1. How satisfied were you with the overall quality of your child's care at _____?

Very Satisfied			Very Dissatisfied	
1	2	3	4	5

2. With which aspects of your child's program were you very satisfied? Please mark no more than 3.
   - _____ 1. Child's teacher
   - _____ 2. Staff in general
   - _____ 3. Physical environment
   - _____ 4. The daily activities
   - _____ 5. Special activities (e.g. field trips)
   - _____ 6. Cost
   - _____ 7. Flexibility of scheduling child's attendance
   - _____ 8. Lunch and snacks provided
   - _____ 9. Other (please specify) _____

3. With which aspects of your child's program were you very dissatisfied? Please mark no more than 3.
   - _____ 1. Child's teacher
   - _____ 2. Staff in general
   - _____ 3. Physical environment
   - _____ 4. The daily activities
   - _____ 5. Special activities (e.g. field trips)
   - _____ 6. Cost
   - _____ 7. Flexibility of scheduling child's attendance
   - _____ 8. Lunch and snacks provided
   - _____ 9. Other (please specify) _____

4. Why did you decide to withdraw your child from the program?
   - _____ 1. Child entering kindergarten
   - _____ 2. No longer convenient because of job change
   - _____ 3. No longer convenient because of change in home address
   - _____ 4. Cost
   - _____ 5. Inability of program to accommodate sibling
   - _____ 6. Dissatisfied with child's care
   - _____ 7. Other (please specify) _____

5. Your child will be:
   - _____ 1. Attending a child care program
   - _____ 2. Attending a family day care home
   - _____ 3. Cared for in his/her home
   - _____ 4. Other (please specify) _____

6. Would you recommend this program as a child care provider for a friend or family member's child?
   - _____ 1. Yes
   - _____ 2. No
   - _____ 3. Maybe

Thank you for your assistance!

Mission Statement

The _____ mission statement expresses the owner or organization's beliefs about how the program is to be run and how it will affect parents, children and the community.

Please think carefully about each question. Then respond with a sentence or two. When you are finished answering the questions, they can become your mission statement.

1. If this program is successful, how might it positively impact the children, families and community it serves?

_____

_____

_____

_____

2. What ethical concerns and practices are employed in this program that might go beyond the norm?

_____

_____

_____

_____

3. What will set this program apart from any other program?

_____

_____

_____

_____

Center Philosophy

The _____ philosophy is a description of the rationale for the educational, disciplinary, and business decisions that you will make. It is also a backdrop for the policies that you create for parents, children and staff. This document should be written very clearly and should correlate with the program mission statement and policies.

To prepare your program philosophy please carefully write answers to the following questions and compile.

1. Is there a known or documented educational philosophy (such as Montessori method or Piaget) that you will use more than most others in preparing curriculum and daily schedules?

_____

_____

2. Describe in your own words the basic concepts of this philosophy.

_____

_____

3. Is there a known or documented discipline philosophy or psychology (such as Behavior Modification or Adlerian Psychology) that you will use more than most others in making guidance and discipline policies and decisions?

_____

4. Describe in your own words the basic concepts of this philosophy or psychology.

_____

_____

_____

_____

5. When thinking about decisions about the business side of the program, do you have a tendency to consider the words or teachings of someone whose ethics or business practices are well known? Describe these beliefs, or your own.

_____

_____

_____

_____

Program Objectives

Program objectives need to be clear, action-oriented statements describing activities that improve the standards of your program, initiate additional program activities, motivate or train personnel, and enhance the experience of the enrolled families.

Objectives must always begin with action verbs. Therefore the sentences have been started for you.
Example: To create an environment that is cheerful.

1. To _____

_____

2. To _____

_____

3. To _____

_____

4. To _____

_____

5. To _____

_____

6. To _____

_____

7. To _____

_____

Organizational Chart

The Organizational Chart is a graphic description of the lines of authority, chain of command, and departments within your program.

Any employee should be able to look at an organizational chart and be able to quickly determine where they are in the organizational structure.

This is the way an organizational chart looks for many child care programs.

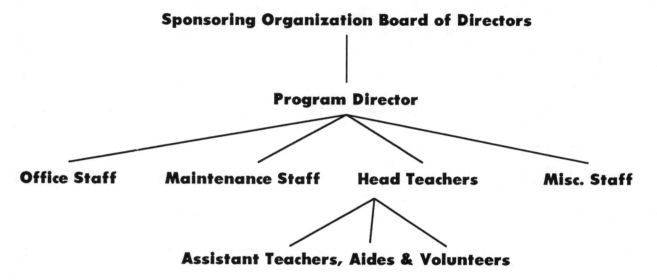

This is a sample. Your organizational chart may look completely different.

Date _____

Name _____ Classroom _____

Please respond to the following question for each category listed.

"If I could change things in our program..."

The staff would _____

_____

The classroom I work in would _____

_____

The management of the program would _____

_____

The children we serve would _____

_____

The parents of the children we serve would _____

_____

I would _____

_____

Additional comments or goals _____

_____

_____

_____

_____

Long-Range Planning Worksheet: Director's Form

Name _____ Date _____

Please summarize staff responses to the following questions.

"If I could change things at our program..."

The staff would _____

_____

The classroom I work in would _____

_____

The management of the program would _____

_____

The children we serve would _____

_____

The parents of the children we serve would _____

_____

I would _____

_____

Additional comments or goals _____

_____

_____

_____

_____

© Early Childhood Directors Association (ECDA) 450 North Syndicate, Suite 5, St. Paul, MN 55104

Dear Parents and Staff,

Each year I like to receive feedback about _____ program. I see this as an opportunity to identify strengths to build on and areas needing attention as we set our goals for next year.

I am asking for the feedback in writing. I am using our philosophy, as stated in our brochure, as the standard by which we are evaluating our program.

I believe the significance of a philosophy lies in the program's ability to operationalize its beliefs.

I hope that you will take time to let us know your thoughts and feelings about our program. What you say is important.

Thank you,

Our Beliefs About Children

We believe that in order for children to thrive, their basic needs must be met.

Therefore: we will provide for the physical and mental health and safety of each child. We shall accomplish this through the establishment of a warm, consistent, and caring environment where children feel secure and can develop a sense of love and trust.

not met   partially met   fully met

Comments:

We believe that children need a nurturing caregiver.

Therefore: nurturing skills will be assessed in hiring staff and utilized in interactions with the children.

not met   partially met   fully met

Comments:

We believe that children need to develop a sense of self-esteem and competence to maximize their potential, and that growth and learning are natural thrusts in human development.

Therefore: we will help children feel that their thoughts and ideas are valued, and we will encourage their expression.

not met   partially met   fully met

Comments:

We believe that children are unique individuals.

Therefore: we will work with each child individually, recognizing personal strengths and weaknesses and encouraging individual potential and growth. Personal competencies will be developed both in individual and group contexts.

not met   partially met   fully met

Comments:

We believe that children need a stimulating, yet orderly and organized, environment to explore.

Therefore: we will provide a rich environment, including attractive interior surroundings, a wide variety of learning materials and play things, and opportunities to explore the natural environment.

not met   partially met   fully met

Comments:

We believe that children have important rights as human beings.

Therefore: discipline and interactions in our program will offer children choices and/or explain reasons for rules and expectations. Since children need to learn self-respect and respect for others, cooperative, considerate, and appropriate behavior will be afforded to and expected from each child.

not met   partially met   fully met

Comments:

We believe that a sense of community is important to social development.

Therefore: we will develop this atmosphere within our program and children, staff and parents by encouraging parental input, teaching children interpersonal skills and placing children in family groupings.

not met   partially met   fully met

Comments:

© Early Childhood Directors Association (ECDA) 450 North Syndicate, Suite 5, St. Paul, MN 55104

Our Beliefs about Learning

We believe that it is important to encourage the development of the whole child.

Therefore: we will provide opportunities for learning that include cognitive, affective, and moral experiences. Individual interests will be pursued as a means to effect learning.

not met   partially met   fully met

Comments:

We believe that for young children, active involvement in the process of learning is as important as specific content.

Therefore: we will provide rich opportunities, encouragement, and support for children to explore the environment and develop, express, and satisfy their curiosity.

not met   partially met   fully met

Comments:

We believe that children need to be able to identify and communicate their feelings, needs and desires, and determine how they can function positively within the context of their social environment.

Therefore: we will assist them to develop important personal and interpersonal skills necessary for social living.

not met   partially met   fully met

Comments:

We believe that cooperation skills are becoming increasingly important in contemporary society.

Therefore: we will provide a cooperative, supportive environment where children will learn to function successfully, first as independent, then as interdependent beings.

not met   partially met   fully met

Comments:

We believe that children must learn respect for others and an appreciation of differences.

Therefore: we will assist them in understanding and enjoying individual and societal diversity.

not met   partially met   fully met

Comments:

We believe that children must learn to make decisions and accept responsibility for those decisions.

Therefore: children will be involved in the decision-making process: identifying the problem, considering alternatives, making a choice, and evaluating the consequences.

not met   partially met   fully met

Comments:

We believe that children must learn problem-solving skills rather than "correct answers."

Therefore: we will teach children to understand and consider different possibilities and to explore alternatives.

not met   partially met   fully met

Comments

We believe that a child's development is greatly enhanced through parental involvement in their care and education.

Therefore: we will communicate with parents on a regular basis; encourage parental participation in our parental education component; and actively seek parental input on important decisions regarding the school.

not met   partially met   fully met

Comments:

Completed by (optional) _____ Date _____

Program:

_____ Infant   _____ Kindergarten
_____ Toddler   _____ School-Age
_____ Pre-School   _____ Nursery School

If you disagree with any of the statements, please comment.

A. Facility

Classroom:

	strongly disagree	disagree	neutral	agree	strongly agree	not enough info.
1. is physically attractive	1	2	3	4	5	6
2. promotes learning	1	2	3	4	5	6
3. has sufficient toys and equipment	1	2	3	4	5	6
4. encourages constructive interaction with play materials	1	2	3	4	5	6
5. encourages constructive interaction among children	1	2	3	4	5	6

Comments:

Outdoor Play Area:

	strongly disagree	disagree	neutral	agree	strongly agree	not enough info.
1. the outdoor play equipment is adequate for large muscle play (balls, jump ropes, etc.)	1	2	3	4	5	6

Comments:

B. Program

Curriculum:

	strongly disagree	disagree	neutral	agree	strongly agree	not enough info.
1. is clear to me	1	2	3	4	5	6
2. provides sufficient opportunities for problem solving in a variety of situations (eg., individual, group, social)	1	2	3	4	5	6
3. provides sufficient opportunities for physical activity and development	1	2	3	4	5	6
4. provides sufficient opportunities for self-initiated activities	1	2	3	4	5	6
5. is challenging enough for my child	1	2	3	4	5	6
6. provides sufficient opportunities for teacher-directed group activities	1	2	3	4	5	6

7. With what aspect of the curriculum are you most pleased?

8. With which aspect are you least pleased?

9. My child seemed to really enjoy and be interested in .....

10. My child disliked....

Comments:

Continued

C. Staff

	strongly disagree	disagree	neutral	agree	strongly agree	not enough info.
Parent-teacher communication:						
1. teacher is approachable and available to parents on a daily basis	1	2	3	4	5	6
2. conferences are of sufficient length to enable me to say what I want to say	1	2	3	4	5	6
3. newsletters enhance my understanding of the classroom	1	2	3	4	5	6

Comments

Teachers, Assistant Teachers and Aides:						
1. appear to respect and enjoy the children	1	2	3	4	5	6
2. appear to understand child development	1	2	3	4	5	6
3. accommodate individual differences in children	1	2	3	4	5	6
4. give the impression of respecting the rights and opinions of parents	1	2	3	4	5	6
5. provide interested parents with opportunities for classroom involvement	1	2	3	4	5	6

Comments

D. Health, Nutrition & Safety:

Illness:						
1. sick children are isolated and cared for appropriately	1	2	3	4	5	6

Comments

Nutrition						
2. Meals are nutritious and adequate in quantity	1	2	3	4	5	6

Comments

Accident prevention:						
1. rooms are safe and free from hazards	1	2	3	4	5	6

Comments

E. Organization and Administration

Director:						
1. she/he is approachable and available to parents on a daily basis	1	2	3	4	5	6
2. respects the rights and opinions of parents	1	2	3	4	5	6
3. policies or policy changes are adequately related to parents	1	2	3	4	5	6
4. she/he responds to your needs within a reasonable time span	1	2	3	4	5	6

Comments:

Fees:						
1. fee schedule is comparable to other centers	1	2	3	4	5	6

Comments

Parents' Form–Program Evaluation (Form 3)

Please check that group that your child is in.....

_____ Infant _____ Toddler _____ Preschool _____ School Age

Please rate the following questions.

low **1**	below average **2**	average **3**	above average **4**	excellent **5**

Is there open communication at _____

_____ a) between you and the director.

_____ b) between you and your child's teacher.

_____ c) If not, how do you feel it might be improved?

_____

Does your child enjoy coming to the program?

_____ a) If not, how could we help make this a more positive experience?

_____

_____ Is the staff accessible to parents?

_____ Is the director accessible to parents?

_____ Is your child greeted in the morning by the staff?

_____ Is your child said good night to at the end of the day?

_____ Does the staff enjoy what they are doing?

Please circle the number which indicates the degree of comfort you generally feel when you leave your child

apprehensive   1   2   3   4   5   feels very comfortable

Is there any way in which we could make the transition easier for you?

_____

_____ Is your child is well supervised at _____

_____ How do you feel about the overall appearance of your child's room?

_____ How do you feel about the overall appearance of _____?

_____ How do you feel about the cleanliness of _____?

_____ What do you see as _____'s major strengths?

What are the areas in which you would like to see improvement?

_____

_____

Please comment on anything else that you feel is important.

_____

_____

Dear Parents,

We are glad you and your child are a part of _____. We know that leaving your child with us can be very difficult. To make this task easier, we want to make sure you feel secure and satisfied with your child's care.

Please take a few minutes to complete this questionnaire. Return the completed form in the attached envelope.

Sincerely,
_____ Child Care Staff

Check the response that best describes your observations and experiences at _____.

	Most of the time	Frequently	Some-times	Never	Not observed
1. The facilities are clean.					
2. There are areas where the children can play individually or in small groups. These areas include art, dress-up, blocks, music, and table toys.					
3. There is enough space for children to play safely.					
4. There are enough toys and learning materials available.					
5. The outdoor play area is safe.					
6. The outdoor play area looks like a fun place to spend time.					
7. My child is greeted when he/she arrives.					
8. Staff members use a friendly tone of voice with my child.					
9. Staff members talk with my child at her/his eye-level.					
10. Staff members nurture my child with hugs, smiles, and gentle touches.					
11. Staff members give directions, using positive words (do's rather than don'ts).					
12. Staff members are consistent in their expectations for my child's behavior.					
13. Staff members know my child personally.					

	Most of the time	Frequently	Some-times	Never	Not observed
14. Staff members are interested in my child's thoughts, ideas and feelings.					
15. Staff members tell my child good-bye when he/she leaves the center.					
16. I am greeted whenever I enter the building.					
17. I am informed of my child's progress.					
18. I am welcome to spend time with my child in the program.					
19. Staff follow through with requests made by me regarding the care of my child.					
20. When I pick up my child, I am able to learn about my child's day.					
21. Staff respond promptly to my questions and concerns about my child.					
22. Staff share their concerns about my child with me.					
23. I am aware of my child's daily schedule.					
24. I am aware of yearly goals for my child's group.					
25. I am informed of special activities and events of the program ahead of time.					
26. I am happy with the way my child spends his/her day.					
27. Important information about the program is communicated on a regular basis.					
28. Program questions about the policies and procedures of the center are responded to promptly.					
29. I can discuss concerns and questions about the program with program management.					

30. I understand program policy regarding

    A. how fees are determined

    B. payment of fees

    C. how vacation days can be used

	Most of the time	Frequently	Some-times	Never	Not observed

Comments

31. How long have you had a child enrolled in _____?

_____ A. less than 6 months
_____ B. 6-ll months
_____ C. 1 year
_____ D. 2 years
_____ E. 3 years
_____ F. 4 years
_____ G. 5 years
_____ H. more than 5 years

32. Currently, I have a child(ren) in

_____ A. Infant Room
_____ B. Toddler Room
_____ C. Preschool Room
_____ D. School Age Room

Thank you for your assistance!

The wishes of the staff summarized on the long-range planning worksheet need to be turned into constructive and attainable goals. Any wish that is really a complaint or a negative statement must be turned into a positive goal or positive wish.

EXAMPLE: "Parents would never pick up their children late." This negative statement needs to be restated so that it becomes a positive wish; i.e. "Parents would always pick up their children on time."

1. List all negative statements/complaints (A). Then rewrite the statement in a positive manner (B). Use more paper if needed.

A. _____

B. _____

A. _____

B. _____

A. _____

B. _____

The next step in the long range planning process is to summarize all of the staff's wishes in the positive format and give each staff member a copy of this list. Allow time for the staff to read them, ask questions, and then brainstorm ways to make these wishes a reality. Give your staff the following example of a staff wish turned into a constructive goal.

STATED WISH:
"That children would be easier to manage on the first day back after a long holiday weekend."
CONSTRUCTIVE GOALS:
1. Send a note home to parents before the weekend describing the problem, ask for their help.
2. Hire additional staff for those days.
3. Plan curriculum and schedules for these days that will meet both children's and staff needs.

When you have finished receiving input from your staff, you need to review their work and finish the task. Your staff involvement at this step is very important since it gives them a sense of ownership to the solution. Next set priorities for meeting these goals.

Goals to be accomplished during the next month:
(you can use other paper for this and write out more than three goals)
1. _____
2. _____
3. _____

Goals to be accomplished three months from now:
1. _____
2. _____
3. _____

Goals to be accomplished six months from now:

1. _____
2. _____
3. _____

Goals to be accomplished one year from now:

1. _____
2. _____
3. _____

Goals to be accomplished two years from now:

1. _____
2. _____
3. _____

The final step is to make sure the goals are written according to a proven success formula, i.e:

1. Have you assigned a deadline for completion of the goals?
   (On monthly goals this needs to be a given day, yearly goals require a month in that year.)

2. Is the goal clear and specific?
   (A goal like "having a nice staff" needs to be described in specific terms that clarify what you envision when you say "nice staff." Example: A staff that communicates clearly with each other and is always friendly to the children and the parents.)

3. Is the goal measurable? Will any person who reads the goal be able to measure whether it has been accomplished?
   (In the goal listed in #2, measurement criteria could be; no more than one complaint from a staff member about another staff person in a six month period.)

These three steps are important to the success of your planning.

© Early Childhood Directors Association (ECDA) 450 North Syndicate, Suite 5, St. Paul, MN 55104

Registration and Enrollment

This section includes forms that will assist you through the various steps involved in enrolling a child in your program. The forms represent the steps from a parent's telephone inquiry about your program to a sample contract for services form.

Please bring all items listed below to the preschool office before your child begins school. The return of all requested items will complete your child's registration process.

As you complete each form, check it off on the list below. This will help to save you time and unnecessary trips to deliver additional materials.

Thank you for your cooperation.

1. _____ Child's History

2. _____ Child's Pre-admission Health History

3. _____ Child's Pre-admission Health Evaluation - Physician's report

4. _____ Identification and Emergency Information

5. _____ Authorization for Release

6. _____ Policies Agreement

7. _____ Parent Rights Statement/Child Abuse Form

8. _____ Emergency Card

9. _____ Parent Volunteer Card

10. _____ Photocopy of Birth Certificate

11. _____ Last Two Weeks Tuition

12. _____ Tuition for _____

Please Note: No child may be admitted to preschool without proof of immunizations. Immunizations received must be listed by your physician and signed by the physician. If you are from out of state or have recently changed doctors, we will need official proof of immunizations before your child may be admitted.

Pre-Enrollment Checklist

Parent's Name _____

Child's Name _____

Child's Group Assignment _____

Attendance Option
    ___ Full-Time
    ___ Fixed Part-Time (specify days)
    ___ Flexible Part-Time

Number of Vacation Days Allocated _____

Number of Personal Days Allocated _____

___Completed Application

___Notified of Opening

    Date Opening is Available _____

    Date Response about Opening Anticipated _____

___Accepted Opening

    Payment Received _____

___Forms Distributed

___Letter of Confirmation Sent

___Pre-Admission Visit

    Date of Visit _____

Staff Parent met with _____

_____

___ Forms Received

    Missing:_____

    _____

    _____

Waiting List Confirmation

Dear Parent,

There is presently no room for your child at our center. Your child's name has been placed on a waiting list. Currently you are _____ on the list.

Please contact me if you have any questions at _____ any time. We will contact you as soon as an opening comes up.

Thank you.

Sincerely,

- -

Telephone Inquiry Form

Date called _____

Name of Child _____

Birth Date _____

Name of Parent _____

Address _____

Home Phone Number _____

Work Phone Number _____

Full Time or Part Time _____

When is Day Care Needed _____

Information Given/Sent to Parent _____

Policies

1. _____ Staff and qualifications
2. _____ Educational program
3. _____ Multi cultural, gender fair
4. _____ Discipline
5. _____ Field first aid/emergency policies and procedures
7. _____ Medication policies and procedures
8. _____ Parent bulletin board and lost and found
9. _____ Parent conferences
10. _____ Parent potluck dinners twice yearly
11. _____ Work days twice yearly
12. _____ Menus, nutrition and mealtime policies for children
13. _____ Bringing gum and food
14. _____ Birthday recognition for children
15. _____ Appropriate clothing and shoes, labeling clothes, extra clothing
16. _____ Naptime, bringing blankets, etc.
17. _____ Use of toy weapons or toys as weapons
18. _____ Bringing toys from home - check with teacher
19. _____ Tuition payment policies, choosing a payment schedule
20. _____ Open staff meetings
21. _____ Day Care Board of Directors

Parents must fill out and return

1. _____ Registration Form
2. _____ Emergency card
3. _____ Health Care Summary
5. _____ Authorization Record

Parents keep for future reference

1. _____ Tuition Payment Policy Sheet
2. _____ Introduction to Day Care Board
3. _____ Program Outline
4. _____ Current Newsletter

Parent Talent Survey

Child's Name_____

Phone_____

We would like to encourage participation in our program. Do you have skills or hobbies you would be interested in sharing with children and staff? We have a few areas listed—please feel free to offer others you may think of.

1. What is profession of mother (guardian)?_____

    father (guardian)?_____

2. How could you help with center field trips?

    ___ Driver. How many children (in seatbelts) could you take? _____

    ___ Chaperone to assist driver or on walking trips.

3. Check ways in which you might be able to enrich your child's days at the center:

    ___ Bring an animal   ___ Play an instrument

    ___ Bring a baby   ___ Teach a special art or craft

    ___ Share a hobby   ___ Put on puppet show

    ___ Share ethnic custom, food, clothing, slides

    ___ Perform science experiments

    ___ Assist with special events, fund raiser

    ___ In-Service for staff

    ___ Other (specify) _____

The purpose in securing this information about your child is to help the child care staff better understand your child and to help you know what to expect from the child care center. Your child's care during the day is a responsibility we share. All information is kept confidential and requires your written permission if it is to be shared. Please use the back sides of form if you wish to elaborate more on a question. Some questions may not be applicable to your child at this time; please leave them blank.

Family and Social History

Telephone _____

Name of Child _____ Birth Date _____

Mother (or guardian) _____ Age _____

Father (or guardian) _____ Age _____

Marital Status of Parents:

Married_____ Divorced _____ Separated _____ Single Parent _____

                          (How Long?)   (How Long?)

Remarks _____

Custody/visiting arrangements _____

Siblings

    Name _____ Birth Date _____

    Name _____ Birth Date _____

    Name _____ Birth Date _____

Other members of the household (include relationship and age):

_____

_____

_____

How long have you lived in this city? _____

Do you speak a language at home other than English? _____

Are there any special words that would help us communicate with your child? _____

_____

Are there any cultural practices or holidays you would like us to know about? _____

_____

Continued

Personal History

Type of Birth: ___ Full Term ___ Premature

Any complications? _____

Age he/she began sitting _____ Crawling _____ Walking _____

Is he/she a good climber? _____ Does he/she fall easily? _____

Age he/she began talking _____ Does he/she speak in words _____ or sentences? _____

Does he/she have any speech problems? _____

Other language _____

Special words to describe his/her needs _____

Sleeping

What time does child go to bed? _____ Awaken? _____

Is he/she ready for sleep? _____ Does he/she have his own room? _____

Own bed? _____ Does he/she walk, talk or cry out at night? _____

What does he/she take to bed with him? _____

What is his/her mood on awakening? _____

Does he/she take naps? (From when to when?) _____

Social Relationships

Has he/she had experiences in playing with other children? _____

By nature, is he/she_____ friendly? _____ aggressive? _____ shy? _____ or withdrawn?

How does he get along with his brothers and sisters? _____

Other adults? _____

With what age child does he/she prefer to play? _____

Will he/she know any children in the center? _____

Do you feel he/she will adjust easily to the child care situation? _____

What makes him/her angry or upset? _____

How does your child show his/her feelings? _____

What method of behavior control is used in your home? _____

What is child's usual reaction? _____

Continued

Who does most of the disciplining? _____

Is he/she frightened by any of the following: _____ animals? _____ tall people? _____ rough children?

_____ loud noises? _____ dark? _____storms? _____ Anything else?

Favorite toys and activities at home _____

Does he/she like to be read to? _____ listen to music? _____

Does he/she prefer to play outdoors? _____ Can your child ride a tricycle? _____

Has he/she had experience with: ___ clay ___ scissors ___ easel painting

___ finger painting? ___ blocks? ___ water play?

Does your child have any other problems that we should be aware of? _____

_____

Health History of Child

What past illnesses has he/she had? At what age?

_____ Chicken Pox _____ Scarlet Fever _____ Diabetes _____ Malaria

_____ HIV _____ AIDS_____ Measles _____ Hepatitis A _____ Hepatitis B

_____ Mumps _____ Other

Does your child have frequent colds? _____

Explain _____

_____ Tonsilitis? _____ Ear Aches _____Stomach Aches

Does he/she vomit easily? _____ Does he/she run high fevers easily? _____

Has your child had any serious accidents? _____ Explain _____

Is child allergic? _____ If so, how does it usually manifest itself? _____ Asthma _____ Hay fever

Hives _____ Other _____ Do you know what his/her allergy is caused by? _____

Has your child ever been hospitalized? _____What for? _____

Has your child ever been to a dentist? _____ Has he had his vision tested? _____

Hearing tested? _____ Does he wear corrective shoes?_____

Does your child have any handicaps? _____ Describe _____

Please give a statement of your evaluation of your child's overall health. _____

Continued

Eating

Is child usually hungry at mealtime? _____ between meals? _____

What are his/her favorite foods? _____

What foods are refused? _____

What eating problems does the child have? _____

Any food allergies? _____

Does child eat with a spoon? _____ fork? _____ hands? _____

Is child left or right handed? _____ What time does your child usually eat breakfast? _____

lunch? _____ dinner? _____ Is family vegetarian? _____

Other dietary restrictions _____

Toilet Habits

Can the child be relied upon to indicate his toileting wishes? _____

What word is used for urination? _____ For bowel movement? _____

Does the child need to go more frequently than usual for his age? _____

Is he/she frightened of the bathroom? _____ Does he/she have accidents? _____

How does he/she react to them? _____

Does child need help with toileting? _____ Was the child easy or difficult to toilet train? _____

Does the child wet his/her bed at night? _____ How often? _____

Briefly describe your child (physical appearance, personality, abilities, etc.)

_____

_____

What are your expectations for your child at the center? In what particular ways can we help your child?

_____

_____

_____

Child _____

Form completed by _____

Date _____

These questions will help us better know and understand your child.

Present dwelling: ___ house ___ duplex ___ apartment ___ mobile home ___ other type _____

___ city area ___ rural areas ____ number of rooms

Has your child moved frequently? _____

Does child have own room? If shared, with whom? _____

What language is spoken at home? _____

What are child's favorite play activities at home? _____

_____

List child's favorite TV programs _____

Does child enjoy music at home? _____ Describe _____

Does child use books at home? _____ Describe _____

Does child have playmates at home? _____

How often does he/she play with other children? _____

_____ same age   _____ older   _____ younger

_____ girls   _____ boys   usual size play group _____

Mother's education _____ Father's education _____

Is child adopted? _____ At what age _____ Does he/she know? _____

Has child had previous group experience (such as play group, nursery school or Sunday school).

If so, describe _____

Does child accept new people easily? _____

Does child undress self? _____ Does child dress self? _____

What makes child angry? _____

Continued

Does child have any pronounced fears? If so, of what? _____

_____

How have you usually handled the fear? _____

Does child have habits, such as nail biting, thumb sucking, temper tantrums, other? _____

If so, describe _____

How do you usually handle this? _____

Does child nap? _____ If so, length of time _____

What is child's attitude about going to bed? _____

Does child have nightmares? _____

At what age was child toilet trained for:

      Urination? _____   Bowel movements? _____

In general, child's appetite is very good, good, fair or poor _____

Does child have strong food dislikes? _____ If so, what? _____

For which hand does child show a preference _____ left hand? _____ right hand? _____ neither hand

How is your child disciplined? _____

Who does most of the disciplining? _____

What are the reasons for disciplining your child? _____

Do the methods you use to discipline your child seem to work? _____

Describe your relationship with this child _____

Describe your child's relationship with his/her siblings _____

What do you like most about this child? _____

What do you enjoy doing together? _____

What do you find most difficult about rearing a child? _____

Has the child's mother ever been separated from the child? _____

If so, when, how long, and for what reason? _____

Child's reaction to separation _____

Has the child's father ever been separated from the family? _____

If so, when, how long, and for what reason _____

Continued

Do any of your family members have a learning disability or physical disability? _____

If so, describe _____

Please describe any special concerns or counseling needed for other family members _____

_____

Please describe anything else about this child or his/her background that might be helpful to the teachers: e.g, ways to comfort child, child's way of communication if speech is insufficiently developed, etc., _____

_____

_____

_____

_____

_____

_____

_____

If the parents are not together:

Has your child had difficulties adjusting to the separation?_____

If so, describe _____

How often does the child see the parent not living with him/her? _____

How does the child feel about visits, if there are visits? _____

Who does the child call "mother," if anyone? _____

Who does the child call "father," if anyone? _____

ADMINISTRATION 43

Child/Family Personal History

Child's name: _____ Date: _____

Height: _____ Weight: _____
Birth date: _____
With whom does your child live?

     ___ Father   Name _____

     ___ Mother   Name _____

     ___ Brothers Names _____

                                _____

     ___ Sisters   Names _____

                                _____

Has your child been cared for by anyone other than parents? _____

If your child has attended another day care, please name _____

Does your child have any history of:
     vision impairment or eye infection?   _____
     hearing impairment or ear infection?   _____
     speech problems?   _____

Has your child ever been tested for a learning disability or developmental delay? _____

Does your child have any special problems? _____

Does your child:
     Have own room?   _____
     Watch T.V.   _____
         How much?   _____
         What shows?   _____

Does your child have playmates? _____

Is your child toilet trained? _____

What words does your child use when wanting to use the bathroom? _____

Does your child need help in dressing? _____

Does your child need help undressing? _____

Does your child have any allergies? _____

Does your child have any special dietary needs? _____

Does your child have any favorite songs? _____

Does your child have any favorite games? _____

Does your child have any favorite toys or stuffed animals? _____

Any other comments which will help us know your child better:

_____

_____

_____

_____

Pre-Enrollment Health Statement

Statement to Physician

_____

Name of child   Birth date

has applied to enter _____. This school provides a program which extends for two-and-one-half hours, two or three days a week. The daily activities include vigorous outdoor play and quiet indoor activities. Please provide a report on the above named child using the form below.

_____

Parent or Guardian

Physician's Report

This report states that the applicant is in good health. It is implied that I have actually examined the child within a reasonable length of time (depending upon the health status of the child). The above named child is under my professional care and to my knowledge is physically and emotionally equipped to participate in the preschool program described above.

Exceptions, if any, are:

Allergies: (name all)

     Animals:

     Bee Sting:

     Drugs:

Illnesses: (Please Check)

     Chicken Pox _____ Measles _____ Rheumatic Fever _____ Hepatitis A _____ Hepatitis B _____

     Mumps _____ Rubella _____ Other _____ HIV _____ AIDS _____ Malaria _____

Accidents or Operations:

_____

Physician's Signature

_____

Date:

Child's name _____ Sex _____ Birth date _____

Father's name _____ Age _____

Does father live in home with child? _____

Mother's name _____ Age _____

Does mother live in home with child? _____

Has child been under supervision of physician? _____ Date of last examination _____

Developmental History

Walked at _____ months. Began talking at _____ months.

Toilet training started at _____ months.

Past illnesses. Check those that child has had and record the approximate dates

Dates		Dates		Dates
Chicken Pox		HIV		Hepatitis A
Asthma		AIDS		Hepatitis B
Rheumatic Fever		Diabetes		Poliomyelitis
Epilepsy		Ten Day Measles (Rubeola)		Hay Fever
Whooping Cough				
Mumps		Three Day Measles (Rubella)		

Other serious illnesses or accidents _____

Does child have frequent colds? _____ How many in last year? _____

List any allergies staff should be aware of _____

Daily Routines

What time does child get up? _____ What time does child go to bed? _____

Does child sleep well? _____

Does child sleep during the day? _____ When ? _____ How long? _____

Continued

Diet pattern   Breakfast _____

                            Noon Meal _____

                            Evening Meal _____

Usual eating hours   Breakfast _____

                            Noon Meal _____

                            Evening Meal _____

Any food dislikes? _____

Any eating problems? _____

Are bowel movement regular?   Yes   No   What is usual time? _____

Word used for   Bowel movement _____ Urination _____

Parent's evaluation of child's health _____

_____

_____

Parent's evaluation of child's personality _____

_____

_____

How does child get along with parents, brothers, sisters and other children? _____

_____

Has the child had group play experiences? _____

_____

Does the child have any special problems - fears? _____

_____

What is plan for care when child is ill? _____

_____

Reason for requesting day care placement _____

_____

Parent's signature _____ Date _____

Date _____

Child's Name _____ Called _____

Birth date _____ Gender _____

Health

1. Does your child seem well most of the time?   Yes   No

2. Is your child taking any medications now?

(Including asprin, laxatives, vitamins, etc.)   Yes   No

If yes, what? _____ Why? _____

3. In a year, has your child had as many as 3 ear infections?

                                                 Yes   No

4. Are you concerned about your child's hearing?   Yes   No

5. In a year, does your child usually have more than 3 colds or sore throat infections with a fever?

                                                 Yes   No

6. Are you concerned about your child's eyes or vision? Yes   No

7. Has your child been seen by a medical specialist?   Yes   No

    If yes, who _____

    Why? _____

8. What arrangements have you made for the care of your child should he/she become ill at the center?

_____

9. Does your child have any handicaps?   Yes   No

If yes, describe: _____

10. Other illnesses or diseases?   Yes   No

If yes, what? _____

11. Does your child have any contagious illnesses that could impact other children or staff (malaria, Hepatitis A, Hepatitis B, HIV, AIDS, etc.)?   Yes   No

If yes, what? _____

12. Has your child been hospitalized?   Yes   No

If yes, describe: _____

Continued

13. Has your child had any serious accidents or poisonings?

Yes   No

If yes, what? _____

14. Does your child chew unusual things such as pencils, chalk, cribs, window ledges, paint chips, plaster or hair?

Yes   No

If yes. describe: _____

15. Has your child had any of the following? Please circle

Premature birth   Trouble breathing at birth

Birth injury or defect   Head injury

Convulsions / seizures

Allergies (eczema, hives, drug, food intolerance, hay fever, wheezing, asthma, insect stings)

Describe: _____

B. Developmental History:

How do you comfort your child? _____

What are your child's favorite toys? _____

What are your child's favorite activities? _____

What language(s) is spoken in your home? _____

C. Sleeping:

Do you have any specific ways of helping your child go to sleep? _____

_____

Does your child cry when going to sleep?   Yes   No

What is your child's current sleeping schedule?

Night time: from _____   to _____

AM nap: from _____   to _____

PM nap: from _____   to _____

Does your child prefer to sleep on his/her   stomach?   side?   back?

Continued

Does your child use a pacifier at naptime?   Yes   No

Does your child use a special toy at naptime?   Yes   No

Does your child use a blanket at naptime?   Yes   No

D. Feeding:

Is your baby breast fed?   Yes No   Bottle fed?   Yes   No

Type of bottle_____; nipple_____; formula_____

Does your baby need to be burped?   Yes   No

What is your child's present eating schedule? (Specify amounts)

	Juices	Food	Milk/Formula
Breakfast	_____	_____	_____
Lunch	_____	_____	_____
Snack	_____	_____	_____

Does your child have any feeding problems?   Yes   No

If yes, what are they? _____

_____

E. Toileting

How frequently does your child have a bowel movement? _____

Appearance of bowel movement. _____

Does your child have diaper rash often?   Yes   No

How is it treated? _____

Child's Name _____ Birth date _____ Today's Date_____

A. Health

1. Does your child seem well most of the time?   Yes   No

2. Is your child taking any medications now?

(Including aspirin, laxatives, vitamins, etc.)   Yes   No

If yes, what? _____ Why?_____

3. In a year, has your child has as many as 3 ear infections?

                    Yes   No

4. Are you concerned about your child's hearing?   Yes   No

5. In a year, does your child usually have more than 3 colds or sore

throat infections with a fever?   Yes   No

6. Are you concerned about your child's eyes or vision? Yes   No

7. Has your child been seen by a medical specialist?   Yes   No

      If yes, who?_____

      Why? _____

8. What arrangements have you made for the care of your child should he/she become ill at the center?

_____

9. Does your child have any handicaps?   Yes   No

If yes, describe:

_____

10. Other illnesses or diseases?   Yes   No

If yes, what? _____

11. Does your child have any contagious illnesses that could impact other children or staff (malaria, Hepatitis A,

Hepatitis B, HIV, AIDS, etc.)?   Yes   No

  If yes, what? _____

Continued

12. Has your child been hospitalized?   Yes   No

If yes, describe: _____

13. Has your child had any serious accidents or poisonings?

          Yes   No

If yes, what? _____

14. Does your child chew unusual things such as pencils, chalk, cribs, window ledges, paint chips, plaster or hair?

          Yes   No

If yes, describe _____

15. Has your child had any of the following? Please circle:

          Premature birth   Trouble breathing at birth

          Birth injury or defect   Head injury

          Convulsions / seizures

          Allergies (eczema, hives, drug, food intolerance, hay fever, wheezing, asthma, insect stings)

Describe: _____

B. Developmental History:

At what age did your child begin to walk _____

How do you comfort your child? _____

What are your child's favorite toys? _____

What are your child's favorite activities? _____

What language(s) is spoken in your home? _____

Has your child been in a group child care setting previously? _____

C. Sleeping:

Do you have any specific ways of helping your child go to sleep? _____

_____

What is your child's current sleeping schedule?

          Night time: from _____   to _____

          AM naptime: from _____   to _____

          PM naptime: from _____   to _____   *Continued*

Does your child use a toy at naptime?   Yes   No

Does your child use a blanket at naptime?   Yes   No

D. Feeding:

What is your child's present eating schedule? (specify amounts)

	Juices	Food	Milk/Formula
Breakfast	_____	_____	_____
Lunch	_____	_____	_____
Snack	_____	_____	_____

Does your child have any feeding problems?   Yes   No

If yes, what are they? _____

_____

E. Toileting:

How frequently does your child have a bowel movement? _____

Appearance of bowel movement. _____

Does your child frequently have diaper rash?   Yes   No

How is it treated? _____

Is your child toilet trained?   Yes   No

What word does your child use for urination? _____

For bowel movement? _____

Does he/she use a potty chair?   Yes   No

Does your child have diaper rash often?   Yes   No

How is it treated? _____

Can he/she easily manage the types of clothing worn?   Yes   No

Child's Name _____ Birth date _____

Today's date _____

Health

Is your child taking any medication? _____ Any allergies?_____

Does your child tire easily? _____

Does he become easily excited? _____

The child's request word or words for using the bathroom _____

Sleep habits: no. of nighttime hours _____ nap _____

Comments _____
_____

Are both parents in good health? _____

Are there any other members of your child's immediate family with a serious health problem?
_____

Does your child have any contagious illness that could impact other children or staff (Malaria, Hepatitis A, Hepatitis B, HIV, AIDS, etc.)? If yes, what? _____

Does anyone help you take care of your child on a regular basis? _____

Is your child right-or left-handed, or undecided? _____

Emotional Background

What type of discipline works best with your child? _____
_____

What previous group experience has your child had, and what were his reactions? _____
_____

How does your child react to babysitters and new people and situations? _____
_____

What kinds of things can your child do by him/herself? (include feeding, dressing alone, washing hands, using the toilet, tying shoes, etc.) _____

Do you have behavior problems with your child? _____
_____

Continued

How do you handle or prevent them? _____

Are you aware of any fears or anxieties your child has? Explain _____

_____

Does your child find it difficult or easy to share possessions with others? _____

Circle the words which best describe your child: confident insecure anxious responsible self-reliant

leader follower cooperative loving fearful

Social background

No. of brothers _____ No. of sisters _____ No. and age of playmates _____

How does your child get along with other children? _____

How much time does your child spend alone each day (excluding TV watching)? _____

Out of doors? _____

Is your child more at home with adults or children? _____

In what situations will your child need the most help? _____

Special interests

Is your child interested in books? _____

What subjects does he/she ask questions about? _____

About how much time does he/she spend watching TV? _____

What are your child's special interests or abilities? _____

What play materials hold his/her attention the longest? _____

    Indoors_____ Outdoors _____

Name and kinds of pets in home _____

Does child have good or poor relationship with pets? _____

Comments: _____

_____

Enrollment Form for Infants

Child's name _____ Birth date _____

Parents' names _____ Home phone _____

Address _____

Dad's work _____   Mom's work _____

Location _____   Location _____

Sibling names and ages _____

Hours and days child will be in day care _____

Please give us information about your child's habits and needs.

Allergies _____

Special Health Conditions _____

_____

Special interests and abilities _____

_____

Comforting needs _____

Communication _____

Naptime habits _____

Eating habits _____

Diet: Type of formula _____ Amt./serving _____oz. times/day _____

Type of food: Amount/serving   Times/day

Cereal   _____

Fruit   _____

Meat/protein   _____

Vegetables   _____

Other fluids   _____
(juices, water, etc)

Have you consulted with a physician concerning your infant's diet?   Yes   No

Parent signature _____ Date _____

I give _____ permission to use wet wipes and over-the-counter diaper rash

ointments on my child as I direct.

Parent signature _____ Date _____

© Early Childhood Directors Association (ECDA) 450 North Syndicate, Suite 5, St. Paul, MN 55104

Starting Date _____ Today's Date _____

Days Attending M_____ T_____ W_____ Th_____ F_____ Hours_____

Child's Name _____Birth date_____

Home Address _____

Phone _____

Mother's Name_____

Employer_____Phone_____

Father's Name _____

Employer_____Phone_____

Child lives with: ___ Both parents

                         ___ Single parent (please name) _____

                         ___ Other (please name) _____

How can parents be reached? _____

Two persons who will assume emergency responsibility for your child if you cannot be reached:

_____
     name   address   phone   relationship

_____
     name   address   phone   relationship

Regular source of medical care:

Doctor _____
     name   clinic   clinic address   clinic phone

Dentist _____
     name   address   phone

Source of emergency medical care:

Doctor _____
     name   clinic/hospital   address   c/h phone

Dentist _____
     name   address   phone

Who is authorized to pick up your child?

_____
      name   address   phone

_____
      name   address   phone

Who is not authorized to pick up your child?

_____

Health

Are there any special health needs the staff should be aware of with your child? _____

_____

Any known allergies? _____

_____

Please explain any special eating habits your child may have _____

_____

Toilet habits

Can your child be relied upon to indicate his/her bathroom wishes? _____

Does your child have toilet accidents? _____

What words does your child use for his/her genitals? _____ for elimination? _____

Social Relationships

List siblings and ages _____

_____

Has your child had experiences in playing with other children? _____

What is your child's nature in playing with other children? _____

What is your child's nature in a group? _____

What is your child's nature alone? _____

What makes your child mad? _____

How does your child show his/her feelings? _____

_____

How do you handle discipline with your child at home? _____

_____

How would you like to see it handled at school? _____

_____

Is your child frightened of anything we should be aware of? _____

How do you comfort your child? _____

_____

What are your child's favorite activities? _____

_____

Are there any special benefits you wish your child to derive from his/her experience with us at the center?

_____

Is there any other information about your child that would be helpful for staff to know to take better care of your child? _____

Parent's signature_____

Full Name _____

Name Used _____ Sex _____

Address _____City _____Zip _____

Birth Date _____Phone_____

Church Affiliation of preference _____

Father's Name _____ Occupation _____

Place of Employment _____ Business Phone_____

Mother's Name _____ Occupation _____

Place of Employment _____ Business Phone_____

Parents are: Married _____ Separated _____ Divorced _____ Other (Explain) _____

Names of other children in household   Age   Sex   Relationship to child

_____

_____

_____

_____

_____

Names of other adults in household and relationship to child _____

_____

Child's previous preschool experience (name of school, dates attended, days per week) _____

_____

_____

Special problems or difficulties with child (health, fears, likes, dislikes, etc.)_____

_____

_____

Persons authorized to take child from school*

_____
name   address   phone

_____
name   address   phone

*Your child will not be allowed to leave the school without authorization from responsible parent or guardian.

I am enclosing the $25 registration and equipment fee which covers registration expenses, the required accident insurance fee, and the purchase of equipment. (Please make check payable to: _____)

It is understood that a two week notice must be given if your child is withdrawn from school.

Parent signature _____ Date _____

Enrollment Form for Nursery School

SESSION: Date _____

T., W., Th. AM (4s & 5s) (9:00-11:30)   _____
T., W., Th. PM (4s & 5s) (12:30-3:00)   _____
M. & F. (3's) (9:00-11:30)   _____
M. & F. PM (4 by Nov. 15) (12:30-3:00)   _____

Child_____

    First Name   Middle   Last   Nickname

Address _____

_____ Zip code _____

Sex _____ Birth date _____ Place of Birth _____ Phone _____

Mother's Name _____

Present Occupation _____ Office Phone _____ Home Phone _____

Father's Name _____

Present Occupation _____ Office Phone _____ Home Phone _____

Marital Status: Separated _____ Divorced _____ Married _____ Single Parent _____

Foster Parent/Guardian _____

Child's Physician _____

Physician's Address _____ Phone _____

Hospital Preference _____ Phone _____

Child's Dentist _____

Dentist's Address _____ Phone _____

Emergency Dental Source _____ Phone _____

Person to be called in an emergency, when parents can't be reached:

Name _____ Relationship _____

Address _____ Phone _____

Name _____ Relationship _____

Address _____ Phone _____

62 FORMS KIT

© Early Childhood Directors Association (ECDA) 450 North Syndicate, Suite 5, St. Paul, MN 55104

School Age Enrollment Form

Please check child care option needed:

_____	7:30-9:00 am	Monday-Friday	_____ $ per week
_____	3:30-5:00 pm	Monday-Friday	_____ $ per week
_____	11:30-1:00 pm	Monday-Friday	_____ $ per week
_____	7:30-1:00 pm	Monday-Friday	_____ $ per week
_____	11:30am-5:00 pm	Monday-Friday	_____ $ per week
_____	7:30am-5:00 pm	Monday-Friday	_____ $ per week
_____	7:30am-9:00 am &		
	11:30am-5:00 pm	Monday-Friday	_____ $ per week
_____	7:30am-1:00 pm &		
	3:30pm-5:00 pm	Monday-Friday	_____ $ per week

Part-time child care (20 hours per week or fewer) hours needed.

Monday _____   Thursday _____

Tuesday _____   Friday _____

Wednesday _____

Total hours needed _____ X $ _____ /hour = $ _____ per week

Weekly rate per this contract $ _____

I understand that any hours or part thereof, that my child uses the center, beyond those registered, will be classified as "drop-in" hours and I will be charged $ _____ per hour for such use.

I understand that if my child is not picked up by 5:00 P.M., I will be charged a $ _____ fee in addition to the $ _____ per hour charge.

Child's Name _____

Signed _____ Date _____

(Parent's/Guardian's Signature)

Enrollment Form for Drop-In

Child(ren)'s Last Name: _____

(Please print legibly)

Child # 1 _____ Birthdate _____ / _____ / _____

Child # 2 _____ Birthdate _____ / _____ / _____

Child # 3 _____ Birthdate _____ / _____ / _____

Child # 4 _____ Birthdate _____ / _____ / _____

Child # 5 _____ Birthdate _____ / _____ / _____

Home Telephone Number _____

Street Address _____

City _____ State _____ Zip Code _____

Child(ren)'s Doctor _____ Phone _____

Child(ren)'s Dentist _____ Phone _____

In case of an emergency:

Persons authorized to take responsibility for my children

Mother _____ Home Phone _____ Work Phone _____

Father _____ Home Phone _____ Work Phone _____

Name _____ Home Phone _____ Work Phone _____

    If parent cannot be contacted

Name _____ Home Phone _____ Work Phone _____

    If parent cannot be contacted

Immunization record

Enter month and year of each dose. Do not use (√) or (x)

Child's name	DPT					Polio				Measles	Rubella	Mumps	HIB
	#1	#2	#3	#4	#5	#1	#2	#3	#4				

I authorize _____ and its employees to obtain medical treatment in an emergency for the above named child(ren), in the event I cannot be reached or am delayed. I give my permission to administer Syrup of Ipecac in the event of an accidental poisoning. I have read and understand the Parent's Policies. I release _____ of any responsibility, except for negligence, for any situation that might arise while the above named child(ren) is at the center. _____ is permitted to use general information about and photographs of the above named child(ren) for promotional use.

Signature _____ Date _____

© Early Childhood Directors Association (ECDA) 450 North Syndicate, Suite 5, St. Paul, MN 55104

Contract for Services

Beginning _____(date) child care services will be provided at our center for
_____ (child's name).

Hours: _____ Days: _____
For the rate of $ _____ . Any care provided for periods other than those stated above
wil be billed at the hourly rate _____.

The weekly rate of $_____ will be paid each Monday for that week's care.

Refunds are not given for center holidays or days the child is absent.
Exceptions:
1. Vacation - If a two week notice is given (written or spoken) to the director, parents pay half the established rate in advance.
2. Severe Illness and/or Surgery, which requires absence of one week or longer, the following rates apply:
      1st week & 2nd week - full rate
      3rd week and beyond - half rate

Sick care is not available. It is a parents responsibility to make subsititute arrangements.

A two week written notice to the director is required to withdraw a child from the program. Parents are responsible for the contracted rate for these two weeks, whether our services are used or not. If it is necessary for the center to terminate this contract, the parent will receive two weeks notice in writing.

When a change of hours, days or payment is needed, a new contract is required as soon as possible.

Parents arriving after the center closes must pay the late fee of $5 per quarter hour. Parents must notify the center if they are delayed beyond their scheduled arrival time.

Deposit: There is a registration fee of $20.00 which must be paid at the time of registration. This guarantees your child a place in the center. It is non-refundable.

Occurences which are contrary to this contract will invalidate the contract and be cause for dismissal of the child from the program.

I (we) understand and agree to abide by the policies and procedures as stated in the parent handbook and the above service contract. I also understand that from time to time the center's coordinator and/or director may implement or change policies as needed. I understand that I will be notified of such changes.

Date _____

Parents _____

Director _____

List brothers and sisters:

Name   Sex   Date of Birth

_____

_____

_____

_____

Experience with other children: _____

How often does the child play with friends? Past or present group experiences (i.e. day care, Y, sunday school,

etc.) _____

Usual routine for napping and sleep:

My child does / does not nap. (Circle one.) Length of time _____

Night sleep: in bed at _____ asleep at _____ up at _____

Toilet training:

What does child say for urination? _____ bowel movement? _____

Discipline:

What discipline practices are used? Redirection, scold, deprive of pleasure, time-out, talking-to, other _____

_____

In what particular ways can we help your child this year? _____

_____

How did you hear about our Nursery School? _____

_____

Medical history:

Allergies, food or other _____

_____

Has child had any abnormal illnesses during childhood? (i.e. continuing ear infections, seizures, anemia, asthma,

throat infections) _____

_____

Has child had any surgery or bone fractures? _____

Continued

Has physician ever been consulted with regard to speech, hearing or vision problems? _____

Are there any health problems in the family? _____

What contagious diseases has your child had? _____

Is your child on any regular medications? _____

If yes, does it alter your child's behavior at all? _____

To complete registration, please enclose the non-refundable registration fee of $30.00.

Parent Participation Commitment

We realize that enrolling our child in _____ means we're concerned about the quality of our child's preschool education.

We are aware of the parent participation requirement at this school. In order for the school to operate in its most productive manner, we will contribute the time and effort to support the school.

We are aware that we will be expected to:

Serve on at least one parent committee in an active way.

Attend the scheduled parent meetings.

Come to school on a rotating basis, depending on class size, to assist the teachers and to bring the snack on these work days.

We will help with field trips either by a) driving a car b) riding with the driver c) caring for the attending parent's children.

We understand that, if we are dissatisfied we may withdraw our child from school after giving the required two weeks notice.

We also understand that the school reserves the right to disenroll a child who does not fit into the school's program, or whose parent does not participate in the cooperative effort of the school.

Signature of parents   _____

_____

Date _____

Financial

This section includes forms that will assist you in developing a financial recordkeeping system. Examples of the forms included in this section are a monthly budget summary form, tuition collection, tuition reminder, petty cash reimbursement form and application for scholarship.

Financial Summary for _____ Center for the month of _____

Expenditures	Month	Last Year	Y.T.D. Cumulative	Budget	% of Budget
Salaries					
Payroll Taxes					
Federal					
State					
F.I.C.A					
Medicare					
Casual Labor					
Contract Services					
Office Supplies					
Office Equipment					
Telephone					
Outside Printing					
Postage					
Program Supplies:					
Art					
Other Cons.					
Program Equipment					
Toys, games					
Other					
Food Costs					
Food Service					
Supplies					
Maintenance and Cleaning					

Expenditures	Month	Last Year	Y.T.D. Cumulative	Budget	% of Budget
Utilities					
Insurance					
Staff Medical					
Dental					
Life					
Property					
Casualty					
Liability					
Student/Accident					
Transportation/Staff					
Transportation/Program					
Staff Training					
Ed. Supplies					
Organizational Fees					
Professional Dues					
Occupancy					

Tuition Collection

Child's Name _____

Classroom _____

Weekly Tuition _____

Vacation Dates _____

Week of	Tuition Due	Field Trip Fee	Lunch Fees	Misc. Fees	Total Weekly Amt. Due	Previous Balance	Total Due	Total Paid	Cash/ Check #	Balance

Late Pick-Up Form

Date _____

To _____

From _____

Re: Late Fee

On _____ you arrived at _____ p.m. to pick up _____. This is after our normal hours. Our late fee is $5.00 for every 15 minutes after 6:05. Your total bill is $_____. Please pay this amount to me immediately.

Thank you

_____

Staff Member

Late Pick-Up Form

Date _____

To _____

From _____

Re: Late Fee

On _____ you arrived at _____ p.m. to pick up _____. This is after our normal hours. Our late fee is $5.00 for every 15 minutes after 6:05. Your total bill is $_____. Please pay this amount to me immediately.

Thank you

_____

Staff Member

Personnel Mileage Reimbursement Form

Name _____   Month _____

Date	Destination	Purpose	Parking	Mileage
_____	_____	_____	_____	_____
_____	_____	_____	_____	_____
_____	_____	_____	_____	_____
_____	_____	_____	_____	_____
_____	_____	_____	_____	_____
_____	_____	_____	_____	_____
_____	_____	_____	_____	_____
_____	_____	_____	_____	_____
_____	_____	_____	_____	_____
_____	_____	_____	_____	_____
_____	_____	_____	_____	_____
_____	_____	_____	_____	_____
_____	_____	_____	_____	_____
_____	_____	_____	_____	_____
_____	_____	_____	_____	_____
_____	_____	_____	_____	_____
_____	_____	_____	_____	_____
_____	_____	_____	_____	_____
_____	_____	_____	_____	_____
_____	_____	_____	_____	_____
_____	_____	_____	_____	_____
_____	_____	_____	_____	_____
_____	_____	_____	_____	_____
_____	_____	_____	_____	_____
_____	_____	_____	_____	_____

Total Miles _____ x _____ = _____ + _____ = _____

(per mile reimbursement)   (parking)   Total Reimbursement

© Early Childhood Directors Association (ECDA) 450 North Syndicate, Suite 5, St. Paul, MN 55104

Cash Tuition Receipt

Received of _____

In the amount of _____

For child care services

Week(s) of _____

Cash Tuition Receipt

Received of _____

In the amount of _____

For child care services

Week(s) of _____

Cash Tuition Receipt

Received of _____

In the amount of _____

For child care services

Week(s) of _____

Cash Tuition Receipt

Received of _____

In the amount of _____

For child care services

Week(s) of _____

Tuition Reminder

Tuition payments are due the first class session of the month. According to our records, your tuition payment for the month of _____ has not been paid or was inaccurate. Please check your records and let us know if we are in error. Otherwise, prompt payment of _____ would be appreciated.

       Thank you,

Tuition Reminder

Tuition payments are due the first class session of the month. According to our records, your tuition payment for the month of _____ has not been paid or was inaccurate. Please check your records and let us know if we are in error. Otherwise, prompt payment of _____ would be appreciated.

       Thank you,

Tuition Reminder

Tuition payments are due the first class session of the month. According to our records, your tuition payment for the month of _____ has not been paid or was inaccurate. Please check your records and let us know if we are in error. Otherwise, prompt payment of _____ would be appreciated.

       Thank you,

Tuition Reminder

Tuition payments are due the first class session of the month. According to our records, your tuition payment for the month of _____ has not been paid or was inaccurate. Please check your records and let us know if we are in error. Otherwise, prompt payment of _____ would be appreciated.

       Thank you,

Unpaid Field Trip Fee

When tallying the field trip money, I did not find a payment for your child. Please check to see if you paid the fee for the following field trip:

Destination _____

Date _____

Amount _____

Thank you for your attention to this matter.

Unpaid Field Trip Fee

When tallying the field trip money, I did not find a payment for your child. Please check to see if you paid the fee for the following field trip:

Destination _____

Date _____

Amount _____

Thank you for your attention to this matter.

Unpaid Field Trip Fee

When tallying the field trip money, I did not find a payment for your child. Please check to see if you paid the fee for the following field trip:

Destination _____

Date _____

Amount _____

Thank you for your attention to this matter.

Unpaid Field Trip Fee

When tallying the field trip money, I did not find a payment for your child. Please check to see if you paid the fee for the following field trip:

Destination _____

Date _____

Amount _____

Thank you for your attention to this matter.

Petty Cash Reimbursement Request

Date of request _____ Name _____

Approved by _____

Item	Purchased at	Amount
_____	_____	_____
_____	_____	_____
_____	_____	_____
_____	_____	_____
_____	_____	_____
_____	_____	_____
_____	_____	_____

Reciept attached

_____ Yes _____ No   Total reimbursement request _____

Petty Cash Reimbursement Request

Date of request _____ Name _____

Approved by _____

Item	Purchased at	Amount
_____	_____	_____
_____	_____	_____
_____	_____	_____
_____	_____	_____
_____	_____	_____
_____	_____	_____
_____	_____	_____

Reciept attached

_____ Yes _____ No   Total reimbursement request _____

Application for Scholarship

Child's name _____ Date _____

Mother's name _____

Father's name _____

Marital status of parents _____ Phone _____

Class at _____ our child is enrolled in (or class we would like our child

to be enrolled in): _____

How many children live with you? _____

What schools do your children attend? _____

Do you pay child care for any of your children? _____

Number of children in child care full time: _____ part time: _____

Is there income from both parents? _____

Please check the appropriate amount indicating your annual household income:

_____ Under $10,000   _____ $25,000-$30,000

_____ $10,000-$20,000   _____ $30,000-$35,000

_____ $20,000-$25,000   _____ Over $35,000

What amount of monthly scholarship would benefit you? $ _____

In exchange for scholarship money I/we are willing to: (example: make puzzles and games, trim soup labels,

do book orders, etc.) _____

_____

Is there any other information that will assist us with our decision? _____

_____

The amount of scholarship money awarded to any one family is determined by the number of families requesting assistance and by the amount of money available for this use. The school will fund up to, but not more than, 50% of a child's tuition. Efforts are made to assist, to some degree, all families seeking scholarships. A committee of board members will make these decisions and notify you as soon as possible.

Personnel

This section includes forms that will assist you in the selection, hiring, and orientation of your staff. This section also includes forms related to substitute staff.

Worksheet to Prepare for Hiring Staff

Position needed _____

Age group or classroom_____

Schedule: ____ pt _____ ft   hours _____

Preferred start date _____

Salary or hourly wage_____

What benefits are available to this person? _____

What type of personality would fit in best with the current staff? _____

Circle the areas that this program could use additional talent, skills, or expertise in:

music   art   science   outdoor activities   storytelling

curriculum development   minority cultures   computers   dance

summer activities   parent relations   languages   reading readiness

language development   gifted education   special needs   Montessori education

CPR certified   other

What are the minimum qualifications I will accept for this position? _____

_____

Application for Employment

Name _____ Date _____

Address _____
  Street   City   Zip

Phone Number _____ S.S. Number _____-_____-_____

Referred by _____ Birth date _____

In case of an emergency, who should we notify? _____

Phone number _____

Employment Desired

Position _____ Date Available _____

Salary Desired _____

What prompted your application with us? _____

Education

Schools Attended   Dates Attended   Major

_____

_____

_____

Would you be willing to continue your education by enrolling in courses or other training programs that may be recommended? _____

Please list any courses, volunteer work, hobbies or interests that would relate to the position you are applying for: _____

_____

Please list any community organizations you are active in: _____

_____

Continued

Former Employers

Name _____ Dates: from _____ to _____

Address _____ Salary on leaving _____

Phone _____ Duties _____

Position _____ Supervisor's Name _____

Reason for leaving _____

Name _____ Dates: from _____ to _____

Address _____ Salary on leaving _____

Phone _____ Duties _____

Position _____ Supervisor's Name _____

Reason for leaving _____

Name _____ Dates: from _____ to _____

Address _____ Salary on leaving _____

Phone _____ Duties _____

Position _____ Supervisor's Name _____

Reason for leaving _____

References

Please list at least three persons, not related to you, whom you have known at least one year who could attest to your interaction with children.

Name	address	phone
Name	address	phone
Name	address	phone

Continued

© Early Childhood Directors Association (ECDA) 450 North Syndicate, Suite 5, St. Paul, MN 55104

Physical record

How would you describe your general health? _____

_____

Have you any defects in hearing? _____ Vision? _____

Speech? _____ Have you ever been seriously injured? _____

If so, how? _____

Describe briefly any previous serious illness _____

Are there any physical or personal limitations on the type of work you can do with children at the center, or that

would affect the amount of time you can spend at work? _____

Date of your last physical exam _____

Would you object to being fingerprinted? _____

Have you ever been convicted of a felony? _____

Do you have a drivers license? _____

Are you available for part time work? _____

Are you available for substitute work? _____

General Information

In compliance with _____ requirements, no person shall be hired or retained as a staff member, paid or volunteer, who has:

a) been convicted of or admitted to or been the subject of substantial evidence of an act of child battering child abuse, or child molesting.

b) used alcohol or drugs such that its effects are apparent during working hours that children are in care, or,

c) been convicted for or admitted to any felony or any offense involving moral turpitude.

I am aware that a background study will be performed before I can be hired.

I authorize investigation of all statements contained in this application. I understand that misrepresentation or omission of facts called for is cause for dismissal.

In the event of my employment with the _____ I agree to comply with the rules and regulations governing my employment. In the event I should terminate my employment, I agree to file my resignation two weeks prior to the date it will be effective. I understand that the first three months of my employment are probationary and if my services have not proved satisfactory, my employment may be discontinued on a week's notice without prejudice.

Applicant's Signature _____

Describe your ideal job: _____

Why do you want to work in child care? _____

What is your philosophy of early childhood education? _____
_____

What is your philosophy of behavior guidance? _____
_____

If hired, what kind of commitment do you expect to be able to give to our organization? _____
_____

What would you say are your goals for the next 1-5 years? _____

What would you say are your goals for the next 5-10 years? _____

If we were to ask your best friend what he/she thought your 5 best qualities are, what do you think he/she would say? _____
_____

If we asked that same person what areas you needed to improve upon, what would they say? _____
_____

What age group do you prefer working with? _____

Is there an age group you absolutely would not want to work with? _____

Describe a positive experience with children, tell what happened and what you think you did to make it positive.
_____
_____

Describe a challenging experience in disciplining children. Tell what you did, and what the outcome was. If you think it could've been handled differently, tell what you would do, if you could deal with it again. _____
_____
_____

Please feel free to add any other comments: _____
_____

Signature _____ Date _____

Start with overview of program, etc.

1. Do you have a degree? What is it? When did you earn it?

_____

2. Have you worked with children? In what capacity?

_____

3. What do you like most about children?

_____

4. What qualities do you feel are important to develop in children?

_____

5. What do you like the least about children?

_____

6. What rules do children need? How would you establish and enforce them?

_____

7. What are your teaching strengths/weaknesses?

_____

8. What is your philosophy of education?

_____

9. Describe what, for you, would be an ideal job?

_____

10. What do you think are the major responsibilities of this position?

_____

11. Are you willing to work with any age group you are not being interviewed for?

_____

12. Why do you think you would be happy in childcare?

_____

13. What are your reasons for changing jobs at this time?

_____

14. What part of your last/present position did you like best/least?

_____

15. How would you describe your relationship with your last supervisor?

_____

Continued

© Early Childhood Directors Association (ECDA) 450 North Syndicate, Suite 5, St. Paul, MN 55104

16. If you had the opportunity what would you change about your last/current position?

17. What are the rewards/benefits of working in this field?

18. When working with others, what is your most outstanding capability?

19. What professional organizations do you belong to?

20. What would your current/former employer say about you?

21. What would your peers at your last job say about you?

22. What activities are you involved in in the community, the church, or in your family?

23. What do you see yourself doing a year from now?

24. What are your long range goals in education?

25. What are your hobbies, special interests, talents?

26. Our goal is to be the best program. What makes a quality program?

27. What kind of commitment do you feel you can make to the program in terms of time?

28. Have you made lesson plans?

29. How would you structure a day?

30. What are your favorite activities to do with children?

31. What are your feelings about touch and what are you comfortable with in terms of touching children?

Continued

32. What are the steps in handling discipline in the classroom?

    What if a child hits?   a child bites?   tips over the easel?

_____

33. What do you do if a child paints himself purple?

_____

34. If you want children to play with playdough, how do you set up the activity?

_____

35. How would you deal with a staff member who uses techniques you disagree with?

_____

36. If you've got 20 children ready to go to the zoo and it starts to rain, what do you do?

_____

37. Have you ever conducted parent/teacher conferences? What is some of the information you convey or expect from parents?

_____

40. How do you communicate with parents at arrival/pick up time?

_____

41. How would you tell a parent their child is a terror in the classroom?

_____

42. What do you feel your relationship role should be toward an aide? an assistant? a parent? the director?

_____

43. What would you do if an irate parent burst into your room?

_____

44. We have a smoke-free environment. Is that a problem for you?

_____

45. Have you ever had experience with child abuse? How would you handle suspected abuse?

_____

46. Is there anything else you feel we should know about you? Maybe
first state as: Tell me about yourself.

_____

© Early Childhood Directors Association (ECDA) 450 North Syndicate, Suite 5, St. Paul, MN 55104

Offer of Employment

Dear

This letter is to offer you the position of _____ at _____.

The starting salary for this position will be $_____ Your first day of employment will be _____

with regular hours of _____ to _____ , _____ through _____ each week.

Extra hours may be available as arranged.

      Benefits and job responsibilities are outlined in the personnel policies and job description which you will receive.

      Please sign below if you have read, understood and accept the offer of a position _____:

program name

please return to the Director.

Sincerely,

Director _____

I have read, understood and accept the offer of a staff position at _____

program name

_____

Signature   Date

Employment Agreement

Employee _____ Age _____

Local Address _____ Phone _____

Permanent Mailing Address _____ Phone _____

Employment Position _____

Term of Employment and Compensation: It is hereby agreed that the employee is employed by the _____

at the rate of $ _____ per _____ for services for a period commencing _____ 19 _____

Conditions of continued employment are outlined in the personnel handbook.

No. of work days per week _____

No. of work hours per day _____

Sick Leave _____

Personal Leave _____

Vacation _____

Salary Increase Agreement: It is impossible to guarantee maximum or minimum salaries beyond the already

approved budget for the existing fiscal year. The _____ - Board therefore reserves the right, at its sole

discretion, to determine what salary adjustments should or can be made during the term of employment.

Attached are the personnel policies and employment practices of _____. The employee

hereby agrees to fully abide by said personnel policies and employment policies and agrees that said policies shall

form a part of this contract as though fully set forth herein.

IN WITNESS WHEREOF, the parties have subscribed their names hereto this _____ day of _____,

19 _____ .

_____

Employee

_____   _____

Current Personnel Chairman   By

Forms in Personnel File

List of what is in file

Employee Name	Personnel Form	W-4 Form	Application Form	Pre-Employment Medical	Emergency Form	First Aid Certificate	I-9 Employment Eligibility Verification	Background Study	Transcripts/License	CPR Card	In-service	Orientation	Job Description	Performance Appraisals

Staff Orientation Checklist

Please initial each of the following categories as you understand them:

_____ Tour of Center

_____ State Regulations/Accreditation

_____ Program Philosophy and Schedule

_____ Parent Handbook

_____ Health Policies

_____ Emergency Procedures (fire, tornado, blizzards)

_____ Procedures for When and Who is to Administer First Aid

_____ Accident Prevention Procedures (daily prevention procedures)

_____ Medication Policies and Permission Form

_____ Accident Report Form

_____ Job Description

_____ Documentation of Staff Qualification Requirements

_____ Personnel Policies

_____ Time Cards

_____ Continuing Education Hours

_____ CPR Training

_____ Dress Code

_____ No Smoking Rule

_____ Age Group Characteristics

_____ Characteristics of Group to be Working With

_____ Child Care Program

_____ Behavior Guidance Program

_____ Cleaning Schedule and Center Upkeep

_____ Sign-in Sheets

_____ Attendance Sheets

_____ Menu Form

_____ Petty Cash

_____ Employment Agreement Form

_____ Reporting Abuse and Neglect

_____ Background Study

The Director and Head Teacher have covered the above information concerning procedures and policies included in each category. I have read and understand the material presented to me.

Signature _____ Date _____

Infant Staff Classroom Orientation Checklist

Be sure to discuss any questions or comments you may have with your supervisor.

Do You Know:

_____ how parents should punch in and out? (special pick-up procedures?)

_____ how to set up and carry out the lunch and snack procedures?

_____ how to carry out nap procedures?

_____ how to clean up after snacks and lunch? (in infant rooms?)

_____ the diapering procedure?

_____ where children's extra clothes and diapers are located?

_____ the procedure for children who borrow diapers/clothes/food?

_____ when and how to sanitize toys and equipment?

_____ what is on the infant cleaning record and how to record completed tasks?

_____ what cleaning is done daily and where that list is posted?

_____ where to find the children's food chart?

_____ where the children's files are located and what they include?

_____ how to fill out attendance sheets?

_____ how to fill out daily report sheet?

_____ where the records and musical instruments are stored?

_____ how to record wets, BM's, diaper rash etc., in changing room?

_____ where completed daily records are kept?

_____ where to find the bottle preparation chart?

_____ where to record when an infant needs more supplies? (i.e. food, extra clothes?)

_____ what your responsibilities are as you come on and go off a shift?

_____ when the sanitizer buckets are to be changed?

_____ what is expected of you in greeting children and parents as they arrive and depart?

_____ how to properly use the microwave and its restrictions?

_____ where children's charts are posted? (parent permission, medications, birthdays, allergies, etc.?)

_____ the procedure for food preparation? food storage?

Preschool/Toddler Classroom Orientation Checklist

Read through the list below to see where you may have questions. Discuss any questions you have with the Director.

Do You Know:

_____ how parents should sign in and out? (special pick-up procedures)

_____ how to set up and carry out the lunch procedures?

_____ how to carry out the nap procedures?

_____ how to clean up after snacks and lunch?

_____ the procedure for toileting and toileting accidents? (preschool)

_____ the procedure for diapering and toileting children? (toddler)

_____ the procedure for brushing teeth?

_____ where extra clothes are located?

_____ the procedure for children who borrow clothes? (diapers/toddlers)

_____ the rules for walks outdoors and field trips?

_____ how to sanitize toys and equipment?

_____ the rules for the sandbox, waterplay tub, record players, painting easel, the reading loft and the play dough equipment?

_____ where extra supplies for the house corner are stored?

_____ where the dramatic play materials are stored?

_____ where to find cognitive materials?

_____ where the musical instruments are located?

_____ the clean-up procedure following an activity?

_____ how to mix paint for easel?

_____ where art materials are stored?

_____ where children's personal files are located?

_____ where the weekly lesson plans are posted?

_____ how to complete daily records for children?

_____ where seasonal room decorations are stored?

_____ where the Saturday procedures, schedules and checklists are?

_____ the rules for personal blankets and "comfy's" that are brought to the center?

_____ where children's charts are posted? (food allergy, parent permission, medication permissions, birthdays, children's schedules, sunscreen?)

_____ how to fill out nutrition and attendance sheets?

_____ how to carry out the Three Threads?

_____ the procedure for caring for a child who is ill?

Continuing Education Request Form

A written request must be made on this form and submitted to _____ prior to attendance.

The course and/or workshop which I would like to attend is: _____

The course is being conducted/sponsored by: _____

This course will benefit me in my job at the _____ because: _____
_____

The date and times of the course are: _____

The training will take place at: _____

The cost of the course is: _____

Supervisor's approval _____   Date _____

Employee's signature _____   Date _____

Approved by _____   Date _____

Send to _____ for personnel file purposes.

Continuing Education Literature Or Tape Review

Continuing Education

Staff Member Signature: _____ Date: _____

Name of Book/Article/Tape: _____

(if Article, name of the Journal)_____

Author: _____   Publisher & Copyright Date: _____

Number of Pages: _____   Length of Tape: _____

Reading Time: _____

Please answer the following questions on the back of this page.

1. What are the main points the author or tape presents?

2. What new insights have you gained from this book/article/tape?

Hours of training time accrued from this project _____

(to be completed by Director)

Warning Notice

Name _____ Date _____

Job Description _____ Branch _____

The _____ Center desires to give all employees every reasonable opportunity to correct unsatisfactory work or unsatisfactory conduct of a correctable nature if the employee evidences an earnest desire to improve. This warning notice now becomes a matter of record, and you will have an opportunity to correct the condition described below.

Any repetition or continuation of conduct or action on your part which is contrary to established rules and regulations, or which is detrimental to the best interests of the _____ or its employees, will result in suspension from employment without pay, or termination of employment.

Reason for this Warning Notice _____

_____

_____

_____

_____

_____

I have read and understand the above.

_____   _____
Employee's Signature   Director's Signature

Prepare in triplicate. Insert the original in the employee's folder. The first carbon should be given to the Personnel Office, and the second carbon should be given to the employee.

Substitute Teacher Information Form

Name _____

Address _____

_____

Telephone _____

Sessions Available   Monday Morning _____   Afternoon _____

                           Tuesday Morning _____   Afternoon _____

                           Wednesday Morning _____   Afternoon _____

                           Thursday Morning _____   Afternoon _____

                           Friday Morning _____   Afternoon _____

Exceptions to above _____

Training:

Degree, certificate or credential earned _____

Year _____

Certificate number, if applicable _____

Expiration date _____

Accredited Child Development Training Courses

Name of Course	School	Date	Hours	Credits

Name _____ Phone _____

Address _____

How early in the morning may we call you? _____
How late at night may we call you? _____
Substitute Level: (Please check those that pertain to you)

     _____ Infant Teacher: day care qualified
     _____ Toddler Teacher: day care qualified
     _____ Preschool Teacher: day care qualified
     _____ School Age Teacher: day care qualified

     _____ Assistant Teacher

     _____ Child Care Aide

Programs you are willing to work with:

     _____ Infant Program
     _____ Toddler Program
     _____ Preschool Program
     _____ Schoolage Program

Hours you could be available to help: _____
Do you have any special considerations we should be aware of (i.e. days you would be available, or guarantee

of certain number of hours, etc.)

_____

_____

_____

_____

Parental Consent

This section includes forms that parents sign allowing their child to participate in your program.

Enrollment Agreement

1 understand that my child is enrolled at _____,

scheduled to begin _____(date and time). If for any reason I choose not

to start on the above date, I must give two weeks notice or I will be charged for two weeks of care for my child.

I also agree that if I decide to withdraw my child, I will give two weeks written notice or be billed for the

equivalent hours.

Parent's Signature _____

Date _____

Enrollment Agreement

1 understand that my child is enrolled at _____,

scheduled to begin _____(date and time). If for any reason I choose not

to start on the above date, I must give two weeks notice or I will be charged for two weeks of care for my child.

I also agree that if I decide to withdraw my child, I will give two weeks written notice or be billed for the

equivalent hours.

Parent's Signature _____

Date _____

Child's Name _____

Child's Address _____
                          Street   City

Child's Home Phone _____

Mother's Name _____

Mother's Address (if different from child's) _____
                                              Street   City

Mother's Home Phone (if different from child's) _____

Mother's Place of Employment _____

Mother's Work Phone Number _____

Phone where Mother can be contacted when child is in the program _____

Father's Name _____

Father's Address (if different from child's) _____
                                             Street   City

Father's Home Phone (if different from child's) _____

Father's Place of Employment _____

Father's Work Phone Number _____

Phone where Father can be contacted when child is in the program _____

Who will be dropping your child off in the morning?

Name _____ Relationship _____

Who will be picking your child up in the afternoon?

Name _____ Relationship _____

Who else has your permission to take your child from the program?

Name _____ Relationship _____

Name _____ Relationship _____

Continued

Who does not have your permission to take your child from the program?

Name _____ Relationship _____

Name _____ Relationship _____

PLEASE NOTE: A copy of the court decision must be on file in order for the program NOT to release a child to his/her noncustodial parent.

Who should the program contact in case of an emergency?

Name _____Relationship _____ Phone Number _____

Name _____Relationship _____ Phone Number _____

Physician's Name _____ Phone Number _____

Address _____

Dentist's Name _____ Phone Number _____

Address _____

Clinic/Hospital _____ Phone Number _____

Address _____

Last DPT _____ Allergies _____ Medications _____

_____

I give permission to _____ to use whatever emergercy measures are judged necessary for the care and protection of my child while under their supervision.

In case of a medical emergency, I understand that my child will be transported to an appropriate medical facility by the local emergency unit for treatment if the local emergency resource deems it necessary.

It is understood that in some medical situations, the staff will need to contact the local emergency resource before the parent, child's physician and/or other adult acting on the parent's behalf.

Parent_____ Date_____

Emergency Authorization Form

Child's Name _____   Home Phone _____

Birth Date _____   Child's Soc. Sec # _____

Mother's Name _____   Father's Name _____

Employed At _____   Employed At _____

Bus. Phone _____   Bus. Phone _____

Names of friends or relatives to call, if you cannot be reached:

1. _____   Phone _____ or _____

2. _____   Phone _____ or _____

Physician to be called in an emergency:

1. _____   Phone _____ or _____

2. _____   Phone _____ or _____

Dentist to be called in an emergency:

1. _____   Phone _____ or _____

I hereby grant permission for the director or supervisors staff person to take whatever steps may be necessary to obtain emergency medical care if warranted. These steps may include, but are not limited to, the following:

1. Attempt to contact a parent or guardian.

2. Attempt to contact the child's physician.

3. Attempt to contact a parent through any of the persons listed on the emergency information form you completed for us.

4. If we cannot contact you or your child's physician, we will do any or all of the following: (a) Call another physician or paramedics, (b) call an ambulance, (c) have the child taken to an emergency hospital in the company of a staff member.

5. Any expenses under 4, above, will be borne by the child's family.

Date _____ Signature _____
                                        (parent or legal guardian)

Subscribed and sworn to before me this _____ day of 19 _____

Notary Public _____

Release of Liability

This release is made by _____
(parent/guardian's name)

whose address is _____

as the parent/guardian of _____
(child's name)

of the same address.

In consideration of the permission granted by _____, to attend _____ and participate in the activities herein, I hereby release and discharge _____, its agents, employees and officers from all claims, demands, actions, judgements and executions which the undersigned's heirs, executors, administrators and assigns may have or claim to have against its successors or assigns to all personal injuries known or unknown, and injuries to property caused by or arising out of the above described attendance and activities.

_____
(parent/guardian signature)

_____
(witness)

Pick-Up Authorization

The people listed below have my authorization to pick up my child from the program. I will inform my child's director/teacher, each time a special pick-up is necessary.

_____
       Name   Relation to Child   Phone Number

_____
       Name   Relation to Child   Phone Number

_____
       Name   Relation to Child   Phone Number

These people are NOT allowed to pick up my child.

_____
       Name   Relation to Child

_____
       Name   Relation to Child

Child's Name _____ Date _____

Parent's Signature _____

Pick-Up Authorization

We must have on file in the office a list of persons who are authorized to pick up each child enrolled. Please fill in the appropriate blanks below:

Child's Name   _____

Carpool Driver(s)   _____

                      _____

                      _____

Child Care Provider _____

Others   _____

                      _____

                      _____

Signed _____ Date _____

Behavior Guidance: Toddlers

The staff at _____ shall provide each child with guidance that helps the child acquire a positive self-concept and self-control, and teaches acceptable behavior. Discipline and behavior guidance used by each caregiver will at all times be constructive, positive and suited to the age of the child.

The following standards and rules will apply in the program for toddler care.

1. To prevent unacceptable behavior from occurring, the staff will:
   a. model appropriate behavior for the toddlers
   b. arrange the classroom environment to enhance the learning of behaviors that are acceptable
   c. use descriptive praise when appropriate behavior is occurring (i.e. "Look how high you're building the blocks! Let's count them.")

2. When unacceptable behavior is about to occur/is occurring, the staff will use:
   a. redirection: substituting a positive activity for a negative activitiy
   b. distraction: change the focus of the activity or behavior
   c. active listening: to determine the underlying cause of the behavior
   d. separation from the group: this is only used when the less intrusive methods have been tried and the behavior of the child is dangerous to him/herself or the other children. In the event that time out is used the child will remain in sight and hearing of the staff. The child will be separated from the group for a maximum time of 2 minutes.

3. Holding and rocking of the child will be done when needed.

_____ complies with all federal, state and other relevant laws which prohibit corporal or abusive punishment in day care settings. Additionally, staff are expressly prohibited from using unproductive or shaming methods of punishment.

_____ believes that parents and child care staff must work together to deal with persistent behavioral issues such as biting, unusual or dangerous aggression, or other issues. Parents will be contacted for a conference when a child appears to be unusually stressed, anxious or otherwise motivated to engage in negative behaviors.

I have read and understand this document.

Signed _____ date _____
           Parent/Guardians

Behavior Guidance

Children are not expected to immediately understand or fully comply with all of the rules; rather, they are to be gently taught, reminded and when necessary, redirected. The staff have the responsibility to set up the environment to encourage cooperation and sharing, rather than promoting aggressive behaviors.

There are times when children, because they are "testing the limits," may actually endanger themselves or others by their actions. Due to these actions, specific behavior guidance steps have been set up and will be followed by the staff. These are:

Logical Consequences

A child who damages a toy, for instance, may be prohibited from the use of that toy for the play period in question. A child who intentionally spills or throws food will be required to assist in the clean up of the spill.

Verbal Reprimand

These are brief verbal behavioral guidance measures consisting of a statement of the problem behavior, the fact that it is unacceptable, and the statement of the acceptable alternative.

Time Out

At times a child may require time to himself to calm down and redirect his thinking. When a time out is given, the child remains within sight of the staff, and the time out is no longer than necessary, and no longer than the age of the child in minutes (i.e. for a 4 year old it wouldn't be longer than 4 minutes). Every time a child is given a time out it will be recorded on a separation report. We will notify the parents if the child has three or more time outs in one day, or five times or more in one week or eight times or more in a two week period. Parents may request to see the separation report at any time.

_____ complies with all federal, state and other relevant laws which prohibit corporal or abusive punishment in child care settings. Additionally, staff are expressly prohibited from using unproductive or shaming methods of punishment.

_____ believes that parents and child care staff must work together to address persistent behavioral issues such as biting, unusual or dangerous aggression, or other issues. Parents will be contacted for a conference when a child appears to be unusually stressed, anxious or otherwise motivated to engage in negative behaviors.

I have read and understand this document.

Signed _____ date _____
      Parent or guardian

Parental Agreement (Form 1)

1. I understand that _____ will not request information concerning my child from any agencies without my written consent.

2. In case of accident of injury to my child, I understand that the _____ staff will contact me immediately. If I am not available, the program may contact the friends, neighbors, or relatives who I have indicated should be contacted in emergency situations. I have provided the program with the names and phone numbers of the individuals who may be called in emergencies.

If none of the above people are available, I authorize the program staff to have my child transported to _____ Hospital for treatment.

This authorization applies to each and every day that my child is cared for by the _____ program staff including days on which car trips, picnics, or other excursions are a part of the programming activities.

3. If I am to request _____ staff to give medication to my child while at the program, I must provide the program with a completed medication authorization form signed by me.

4. These arrangements are in effect as long as my child is enrolled in the program or unless I notify the program, in writing, of my cancellation.

Child's Name _____

Parent's Signature _____

Date _____

I hereby grant permission for my child to use all of the play equipment, and participate in all of the activities of the center.

I hereby grant permission for my child to leave the program under proper supervision for neighborhood walks.

I hereby grant permission for my child to be included in evaluations and pictures connected with the program.

I hereby grant permission for the Director or Acting Director to take whatever steps that may be necessary to obtain emergency medical care for my child if warranted. These steps may included, but are not limited to, the following:

1. Attempt to contact a parent or guardian.

2. Attempt to contact the child's physician.

3. Attempt to contact the parent through any of the persons listed by the parent on the emergency medical form.

4. In the event that #1 - #3 are unsuccessful:
    A) Call another physician
    B) Call the paramedics
    C) Have the child taken to an emergency hospital

I understand that any expenses incurred under #4 above will be borne the child's family.

Child's Name _____

Mother's Signature _____

Date _____

Father's Signature _____

Date _____

Parental Agreement (Form 3)

Permission Form for _____ Dated _____

Syrup of Ipecac

Ipecac is a drug extracted from the Ipecacuana plant of South America. It is a natural irritant to the stomach which safely induces vomiting in twenty minutes. If a poison has accidentally been ingested, it may need to be removed to prevent absorption.

I hereby give my permission to the _____ staff to administer Syrup of Ipecac to my child after consultation with the Poison Control Center.

signed _____

Emergencies

I hereby give my permission to the _____ staff to act in a medical emergency situation and for appropriate medical staff to administer emergency medical treatment to my child.

signed _____

Impromptu Walks

I hereby give my permission for my child to go on impromptu walking field trips in the neighborhood. This includes walks around the block, (list specific parks, etc.) the Fire Hall and the adjoining neighborhood.

signed _____

Photographs

I do _____ I do not _____ give my permission for my child to be photographed in the program, program functions and field trips and the photographs to be displayed. I understand that the photographs may be taken by school staff, professional photographers, news media or other parents. I understand that I will be notified if any photos are to be used for publicity purposes and that I have the right to refuse permission.

signed _____

Parental Agreement Form (Form 4)

Child's Name _____ Class _____

Please check "yes" or "no" to the following statements, sign your name and return one copy to the center and keep the copy in the Policies and Procedures Handbook for your records.

	YES	NO
1. I have received the _____ Handbook.	_____	_____
2. I have been informed of and understand, the policies and procedures of _____	_____	_____
3. I have been informed of the goals and overall program of _____.	_____	_____
4. I am aware that I will be informed of specifics through a monthly newsletter.	_____	_____
5. I have received and returned a Health Form stating the dates of my child's immunizations.	_____	_____
6. If the response to Statement 5 is "No," I will submit the Health Form within two weeks.	_____	_____
7. I agree that it is the responsibility of both the staff of _____ and I/we as parent(s) to keep an open line of communication between us during the school year.	_____	_____
8. I understand that all parents will be asked to evaluate the program, in the spring using the form provided.	_____	_____
9. I understand there wll be two written evaluations of my child during the school year and two Parent-Teacher Conferences.	_____	_____
10. I give my permission to have my child's picture used for publicity purposes.	_____	_____
11. My child may be identified by name in any picture used for publicity purposes.	_____	_____
12. I understand that tuition payments are due on the first of the month and that if they are not received by that date, a late fee will be added to my amount due.	_____	_____
13. I understand that there is a late pick-up fee once the door is locked following dismissal.	_____	_____
14. I have provided the school with all written information that has been requsted.	_____	_____

Date _____
Parent/Guardian signature

Parental Agreement (Form 5)

YES   NO

_____ _____   I hereby grant permission for my child to use all of the play equipment and participate in all activities of the program.

_____ _____   I hereby grant permission for my child to leave the program premises under the supervision of a staff member for neighborhood walks.

_____ _____   I hereby grant permission for my child to be included in evaluations or research activities approved by the director.

_____ _____   I hereby grant permission for my child's name or picture to be used in publicity connected with the program.

I understand the center will not be responsible for anything that may happen as a result of false information given at the time of enrollment.

I authorize the following persons to take my child from the center and agree to give written permission if my child is to be released to anyone not listed below. (List full names and identify relationship)

_____

_____

_____

_____

The following persons are not authorized to take my child from the center. (List full names and identify relationship)

_____

_____

Date _____ Signature _____

(parent or legal guardian)

Consent for Transfer of Child's Records

Dear Parent,

In order to transfer health forms and send a final report of your child's progress at _____,
we must have on file a written permission form.

The records and report will be mailed directly to the requested school. You will receive a copy of the teacher's report.

Please complete the permission form below.

_____ has my permission to send a progress report and health forms for my

child _____ to:
       child's name

School _____

Address _____

Attention _____

Signed _____

Date _____

© Early Childhood Directors Association (ECDA) 450 North Syndicate, Suite 5, St. Paul, MN 55104

Name Release Form

This release form MUST BE SIGNED AND RETURNED before your child's phone number and address can be included on the printed class roster. Please return it to the program by _____ or give it to the teacher at the home visit. Thank you.

As the parent (guardian) of _____,
                              (child's name)

I give my permission to have my child's name, phone number and home address on the class roster to be distributed to parents of children in the class and to staff and board members.

Parent Signature _____ Date _____

Comments:

Consent for Release of Health Information

Child's name _____

Consent for Release of Health Information

The information contained in the child's record is collected to assist the license holder in providing appropriate care for the child. It is available to the child, the child's parent or guardian, the child's legal representative, employees of the license holder and the Commissioner of the Department of Human Services.

With this release, I permit the health consultant of the license holder to review health and medical information contained in the child's record in order to identify specific health/medical needs of the child and to recommend program plans to assist the license holder meet these health/medical needs.

Signature of Parent/Legal Guardian _____ Date _____

© Early Childhood Directors Association (ECDA) 450 North Syndicate, Suite 5, St. Paul, MN 55104

Emergency Card

Name _____ Birthdate _____

Address _____

Parents:

Telephone Numbers:

_____ (home) _____

(work) _____

_____ (home) _____

(work) _____

Emergency Contacts: (name/address/phone)

_____

_____

Medical Care: (name/address/phone)

Physician _____

Dentist _____

Significant Medical Information _____

_____

I give permission to _____ to make whatever emergency measures are judged necessary for the care and protection of my child while under the supervision of the program.

In case of a medical emergency, I understand that my child will be transported to _____ by the local emergency unit for treatment, at my expense, if the local emergency resource (Police, Rescue Squad) deems it necessary.

In the event of an accidental ingestion, I understand that_____ will contact the Poison Control Center. I give my permission for the staff to administer Syrup of Ipecac to my child if directed to do so by Poison Control.

I hereby authorize _____ to act on my behalf in case of an emergency.

Parent's signature _____ date _____

Consent for the Use of Syrup of Ipecac

Poisons can be defined as any agent that kills, injures or impairs a living organism. Each year approximately 3,000,000 poisonings occur throughout the nation. Eighty percent of these involve children under the age of five. This statistic is not surprising if one considers that young children have curious, exploring personalities and little knowledge of toxic substances.

_____ has taken every precaution to ensure that potential poisons are out of the reach of the children we care for. In the event that an accidental ingestion should occur, however, our staff will consult with the Poison Control Center. If vomiting is the recommended course of treatment, our center will administer Syrup of Ipecac as instructed by Poison Control.

Syrup of Ipecac could save your child's life in an accidential ingestion. This medicine can be bought in any pharmacy without a prescription. It is used to induce vomiting when it is desirable to empty the stomach quickly to prevent further absorption of the poison. *Ipecac would never be used without the recommendation from Poison Control.* This medicine comes in liquid form and is given with water, juice or pop. One staff person would stay with your child to observe his/her condition and help him/her through this process. As a parent/guardian, you would be notified immediately of the poisoning, information provided by Poison Control as well as their recommendations for treatment and the condition of your child.

In the event of an accidental ingestion, I understand that the staff will contact the Poison Control Center. I give my permission for the staff to administer Syrup of Ipecac to my child if directed to do so by the authorities at Poison Control.

Signature of Parent/Guardian _____ Date _____

Consent for Non-Prescription Medications

Child's name _____

I hereby give _____ permission to apply any of the following external preparations that are checked, in accordance with directions for use on the appropriate container:

_____ Soap
_____ Baby Wipes
_____ Baby Lotion
_____ Baby Powder
_____ Baby Oil
_____ Non-prescription ointments (such as Desitin, Vaseline)
_____ Teething Gel
_____ Fever-reducing medication (such as Tylenol)
_____ Other - please specify _____

Signature, Child's physician _____

Signature, Child's parent _____ Date _____

Child's Name _____

Date	Medication Administered	Amount Given	Time Given	Initials

Medication Permission Sheet (Form 1)

Child's Name _____

Date _____

Medication _____ exp. date _____

Reason for medication _____

Instructions for use _____

_____

Dosage & Time _____

I request the above medication be given to my child as prescribed.

Date _____ Signature _____

Dr. Name _____ Clinic _____

Phone _____

Child's Pharmacy _____

Phone _____

Program Staff:
Fill in date, time and dosage whenever you dispense this medication. Your signature and name must accompany this information.

Medication returned to parents on _____
(please place this form in the child's folder when medication is complete)

Medication Permission Sheet (Form 2)

(to be filled out by parent or physician)

Child's name _____ Date _____

All medication to be administered by day care staff must be authorized by parent's signature. (Physician's signature optional)

I have prescribed the following medication for this child and request that dosage falling during child care hours be administered by child care program personnel.

If more than one medication, please fill out separate sheet for each.

Medication _____ Condition for which prescribed _____
Special side effects to be aware of (if any) _____
Instructions for use (at least note time and dosage) _____
How long? Please circle: Until used up   Will notify daily.

If notifying daily, please write in which dates as they occur and initial

_____   _____   _____   _____   _____   _____   _____   _____   _____   _____

Signed _____   Signed _____
　　　　　　　　　Parent　　　　　　　　　　　　　　　　　　Physician (optional)
Phone _____   Phone _____

Pharmacy _____ Phone _____ RX# _____
Program staff fill in date, time and initials whenever dispensing medicine.

| Monday | | | Tuesday | | | Wednesday | | | Thursday | | | Friday | | |
Date	Time	Intl	Date	Time	Intl	Date	Time	Intl	Date	Time	Intl	Date	Time	Intl

| Saturday | | |
Date	Time	Intl

Disposition of Medicine. Please Circle One:

Used Up　　　　　　Threw Away

Gave Back to Parent

(each day)

Please place this form in the child's folder when medication is complete.

Field Trip Permission Form

Date of Trip _____

Destination _____

Cost _____

Child's name   Parent's signature

1. _____

2. _____

3. _____

4. _____

5. _____

6. _____

7. _____

8. _____

9. _____

10. _____

11. _____

12. _____

13. _____

14. _____

15. _____

16. _____

17. _____

18. _____

19. _____

20. _____

21. _____

22. _____

Field Trip Permission Form

My child, _____, has my permission to participate in any field trips planned by his/her teachers at the program. I understand that individual seat belts will be used for each child when traveling by car or van, and that adequate supervision will be provided during the entire trip. I also understand that only qualified drivers will be asked to drive.

Signed _____ Date _____

_____ I would be interested in helping provide transportation for a field trip.

My car has _____ seatbelts available for passengers.

Field Trip Permission Form

My child, _____, has permission to go by (car, van, bus) to _____
                                                                                      (destination)
with the program on _____
                                  (date)

Parent's signature _____ Date _____

Personnel Files

This section includes forms that should help you maintain essential information in each staff person's file.

Personnel File Contents

Name _____

	Year _____	Year _____	Year _____
Application	_____	_____	_____
Job Description	_____	_____	_____
Ed. Verification	_____	_____	_____
Orientation	_____	_____	_____
I-9 Form	_____	_____	_____
Physical	_____	_____	_____
TB Results	_____	_____	_____
Personnel Information Form	_____	_____	_____
Emergency Information	_____	_____	_____
Teaching License	_____	_____	_____
First Aid	_____	_____	_____
CPR	_____	_____	_____
Inservice	_____	_____	_____
Background Study	_____	_____	_____
Performance Appraisal	_____	_____	_____
Contract	_____	_____	_____
Pay Schedule	_____	_____	_____
W-4	_____	_____	_____

Staff person

      Starting date _____

      Starting salary _____

      2 month review _____

3 month review

      Salary_____

      Staff's signature _____

      Director's signature _____

1 year review

      Salary _____

      Staff's signature _____

      Director's signature _____

2 year review

      Salary _____

      Staff's signature _____

      Director's signature _____

Personnel Responsibility Agreement

The completion of the following areas of compliance are the responsibility of the employee. It is required that each staff member will comply in a conscientious and timely manner.

1. Complete and sign a *Personnel Information Form* as required.

2. At the time of hire and every two years thereafter, submit the Personnel Medical Report signed by source of medical care and based on a thorough examination done within previous 3 months.

3. Provide documentation to support qualifications for job position (teacher, assistant teacher, aide).

4. Within the first year of employment, complete an intensive first aid course available through the various community organizations or through the Public Health Nurse. (First aid orientation will be provided at time of hire.) First aid training must be updated by the employee every three years.

5. Complete required inservice training by the end of the 11th month of each licensing year.

Furthermore, it is expected that all staff attend the staff training program held each summer to provide staff with the opportunity to complete substantial hours of training.

I have read, understand and agree to fulfill my responsibilities as outlined.

Employee Signature _____ Date _____

CC: Employee

Personnel Policy Agreement

As a new employee, I have read the _____ handbook and understand what is expected of me in the new position.

I have read the Employee Policies of this program and find them satisfactory.

I have read the Parent Policies and agree to carry them out to the best of my abilities.

I understand the probationary period is to be three (3) months as stated in the Employee Policies.

Although I have been hired for certain hours, I understand they may be changed to meet the needs of the child care staffing ratios.

Although I have been hired as _____ in the room, I understand my assignment may be changed to meet the needs of the child care staffing ratios.

Staff signature _____ Date _____

Personnel Policy Agreement

I have completed an orientation procedure.

I have read all the Policies & Procedures of the program.

I have read all forms which go to the parents.

I have read the personnel policies, understand them, and agree to adhere to them.

Staff signature _____ date _____

Director signature _____ date _____

Staff Emergency Information

Name _____

Address _____

Contact Persons in event of emergency

1. _____
    Name   Relation   Phone

2. _____
    Name   Relation   Phone

Physician _____ Phone _____

Medical Insurance _____

Allergies _____

Medications _____

Hospital _____

Other Significant Information _____

_____

In case of a medical emergency, I understand that I will be transported to an appropriate medical facility by the local emergency unit for treatment if the local emergency resource deems it necessary.

It is understood that in some medical situations, the staff will need to contact the local emergency resource before your physician, and your specified contact person.

Signature _____ Date _____
           Parent or legal guardian

Staff Medical Form

In order to protect both the staff and the children receiving care at _____,
there shall be on file a pre-employment medical record of each staff member. That medical record can consist of
the information asked for on this form,. or a similar form supplied by the doctor, or a statement by the doctor that
shows evidence of acceptable emotional and physical fitness on the part of the employee.

To be completed by the Director/Owner of the Facility:

Name of Applicant _____

Position Applied for _____

Hours _____

Duties and responsibilities will include _____

_____

To be Completed by the Physician:

Some lifting of young children and some picking up and moving of furniture and equipment may be required. Since
we are vitally involved with the wholesome emotional growth of the child, we require good mental health of our
employees. In your opinion, is this applicant free of disease or serious mental or emotional handicaps that would
be detrimental to the children and adults with whom the applicant will be working?

In your opinion, is this applicant free of any physical defect that would prevent the performance of the above listed
duties?

General physical condition _____

_____

Evidence of required tuberculin test:

     Type of test _____ Date _____ Result _____

Date of Examination _____ Signature of Physician _____

Address _____

Phone Number _____

Infectious Disease Agreement

I acknowledge receiving information on the exposure to the infectious diseases that I am susceptible to working in a child care setting. I have been informed of precautionary procedures that I can take, and I am aware of the importance of handwashing and the importance of wearing gloves when in contact with blood or any body fluids. I understand that I will be kept informed of any illnesses present in the program, with health alerts.

Staff Signature _____ Date _____

Infectious Disease Agreement

I acknowledge receiving information on the exposure to the infectious diseases that I am susceptible to working in a child care setting. I have been informed of precautionary procedures that I can take, and I am aware of the importance of handwashing and the importance of wearing gloves when in contact with blood or any body fluids. I understand that I will be kept informed of any illnesses present in the program, with health alerts.

Staff Signature _____ Date _____

Infectious Disease Agreement

I acknowledge receiving information on the exposure to the infectious diseases that I am susceptible to working in a child care setting. I have been informed of precautionary procedures that I can take, and I am aware of the importance of handwashing and the importance of wearing gloves when in contact with blood or any body fluids. I understand that I will be kept informed of any illnesses present in the program, with health alerts.

Staff Signature _____ Date _____

Infectious Disease Agreement

I acknowledge receiving information on the exposure to the infectious diseases that I am susceptible to working in a child care setting. I have been informed of precautionary procedures that I can take, and I am aware of the importance of handwashing and the importance of wearing gloves when in contact with blood or any body fluids. I understand that I will be kept informed of any illnesses present in the program, with health alerts.

Staff Signature _____ Date _____

Maternity Policy Agreement

Working in a child care setting requires you to take precautions against infection. Because germs are more easily spread in a setting where there is diapering, runny noses, drooling, food service and other instances relating to the care of children, it is your responsibility to know and practice the health, safety and emergency procedures as set out by _____

(Program Name)

There are special risks to you if you should become pregnant while working in child care. You are advised to see your doctor before the end of the first trimester of pregnancy.

Please sign below that you have:

1)   read and understand there are risks involved in being pregnant and working in a child care program.

2)   that you will follow the policies and procedures set out by this program to guard against the spread of disease.

Staff signature _____

Date _____

Child Abuse Reporting Form

I acknowledge reading information on the responsibilities of mandated reporters of child maltreatment. I realize that as a child care professional, it is my personal responsibility to report directly to the _____ Department of the affected child's county of residence.

Any reports needing to be made about children at _____ should be made from the Director's office with the Director or Coordinator present. Once the report has been made any conferences that may occur with the family will be handled by the Director.

Signature _____ Employee Number _____

Date _____

Personnel Chemical Exposure Agreement

I acknowledge receiving information and instructions on types, handling and potential hazards of chemicals I may be exposed to in my job. I have been informed of emergency procedures and where emergency phone numbers are posted in the program.

I understand that I will be kept informed of changes in chemicals used. Upon request, additional information about these chemicals is available to me.

Signature _____ Employee Number _____

Date _____

Time Card

Name of Employee _____

Employee Number _____

Date	Arrived	Time Off	Left	Total Regular Hours	Overtime	Total Hours

Signed _____ Approved _____
               (Employee)   (Supervisor)

Grievance Form

Date:

Grievance:

Date of incident:

Describe any immediate action or reaction:

Who was the incident reported to:

Was any resolution made immediately?

If this is something that cannot be resolved immediately send this form to:

_____

Request for Time Off

(Please allow two weeks notice except in cases of illness or death)

Name _____

Date requested _____

Date(s) needed off _____

Hours needed off _____

Charge hours to: _____ Personal time

                             _____ Non-paid hours

                             _____ Sick time

Designation of personal day/hour use _____

(v=vacation; s=sick day; f=funeral; pt=personal time; fh=floating holiday; b=birthday).

Director's use only

Time approved: yes/no

If no, why _____

Number of hours remaining in _____ time account _____

Director's signature _____ Date _____

Cleaning Check-Off List

Week of _____

Initial each item as it is cleaned up for the day:

AREA/ITEM	M	W	F	COMMENTS
Toddler Room				
Vacuum carpet				
Sweep/wet mop floors				
Buff floors (twice week)				
Scrub toilet				
Wipe down bathroom walls				
Scrub sinks				
Empty trash-scrub can inside/outside				
Wipe out window sills				
Wipe down heat registers/air vents/doors				
Hallway				
Sweep/wet mop (buff floor)				
Clean back door window				
Wipe down air vent/heat register				
Buff floors (twice week)				
Preschool Room				
Vacuum carpet				
Sweep/wet mop floors				
Scrub toilets				
Wipe down bathroom walls				
Scrub sinks				
Clean mirrors/paper towel holder				
Empty trash/scrub can inside/outside				
Wipe out window sills				
Wipe down heat registers/air vents				
Clean doors and door frames				
Staff Bathroom				
Mop floor				
Scrub toilet				
Clean sink/mirror/paper towel holder				
Wipe down door and door frame				
Entryway to rooms				
Sweep/wet mop floor (buff floor)				
Main Entryway/Corridors/Stairs				
Vacuum				
Sweep and wet mop floors/stairs				
Kitchen				
Sweep and mop floor				
Clean sink				
Wash wall area behind sink				
Wipe front of fridge				

Recorded Hours

Time

Hours

Number of people

Weekly hours

Signature

Closing Check-Off List

Week of _____   Initial each item as it is cleaned up for the day

ITEM/AREA	M	T	W	T	F	COMMENTS
Downstairs Kitchen/Gym						
Lock refrig. & freezer						
Lock up all toys in gym closet-Fri. only						
Turn off all lights						
Bathroom/Halls						
Flush all toilets						
Turn off all lights						
Lounge						
Close windows						
Turn off all lights						
Straighten up						
Remove pop bottles on Wed. or as needed						
Office						
Close windows						
Lock filing cabinets						
Entryway						
All lights off except lamps						
Lock doors						
Set alarm						
Recheck doors on the way out						
All classrooms						
Close all windows						
Lock deck doors						
Turn off lights						
Straighten/replace all toys/books						
Clean off tables						
Straighten chairs						
Replace borrowed equipment						
Nap room						
Straighten cots						
Turn off all lights						
Friday only/Nap room						
Change sheets						
Correct blankets folded on cots						
Cots stacked						

© Early Childhood Directors Association (ECDA) 450 North Syndicate, Suite 5, St. Paul, MN 55104

Home Visit Form

Child _____ Birth Date _____

Address _____

Home Visit Date _____

          Time _____

Day birthday celebrated _____

Information needed from parent

    _____ Health form   _____ Hospital

    _____ Name Release form   _____ Dentist

    _____ Emergency Names   _____ Registration form

    _____ Doctor

Objective parent has for child:

Parent Signature _____ Date _____

Request for Supplies

Snack or Craft Item	Amount Needed	Date Needed

Person making the request _____ Date of request _____

Maintenance Request Form

Date _____ Classroom _____

_____ Equipment repair needed   _____ Facility repair needed

_____ **This is a SAFETY concern!**

Please give a detailed description of repair needed _____

_____

_____

Repair completed on _____ By _____

Request for Errand Form

Date needed _____

What needs to be done _____

_____

Destination (give specific address if not a regular errand, and name of person to see, if needed)

_____

_____

Name of staff making request _____

Date request submitted _____

Driver's signature _____

Date completed _____

Note: this form should be completed and submitted in advance. A minimum of two days advance notice is required.

Performance Appraisal

In this section you will find forms to assess staff and director competence and attitudes. Included are a variety of forms helpful if you are evaluating a staff person as well as to encourage self-evaluation.

Curriculum

Plans a developmentally appropriate curriculum that is appropriate for the age span of the children within the group and is implemented with attention to the different needs, interests, and developmental levels of those children.

_____ 1. Curriculum provides for all areas of child's development: physical, emotional, social and cognitive through an integrated approach.

_____ 2. Curriculum is based on teacher's observations and recordings of each child's special interests and developmental progress.

_____ 3. Curriculum planning provides an environment for children to learn through active exploration and interaction with adults, other children and materials.

_____ 4. Curriculum is planned to accomodate not only the chronological development of the children, but also to meet the needs of children who exhibit unusual interests and skills outside the normal developmental range.

_____ 5. Curriculum is planned to provide a variety of activities and materials; with increasing difficulty, complexity and challenge.

_____ 6. Curriculum is enhanced and expanded by asking questions or making suggestions that stimulate children's thinking.

_____ 7. Multicultural and nonsexist experiences, materials and equipment provided for children of all ages.

_____ 8. Curriculum encourages creative expression and appreciation of the arts.

_____ 9. A balance of child-initiated/teacher-initiated activities are provided.

_____ 10. Transitions will be a vehicle for learning with smooth , unregimented transitions between activities.

_____ 11. A balance of rest and active movement is provided for children throughout the day.

_____ 12. Outdoor experiences provided for children of all ages.

Curriculum

_____ Needs improvement _____ Adequate _____ Very Good _____ Excellent

Comments:

Children

_____ 1. Responds quickly and directly to children's needs, desires, and messages and adapts responses to children's differing styles and abilities.

_____ 2. Many opportunities are provided for children to communicate.

_____ 3. Successful completion of tasks is facilitated by providing support, focused attention, physical proximity, and verbal encouragement. It is recognized that children learn from trial and error.

_____ 4. Signs of undue stress in children's behavior are recognized and there is an awareness of appropriate stress-reducing activities and techniques.

_____ 5. The development of self-esteem is facilitated by respecting, accepting and comforting child regardless of the child's behavior.

_____ 6. Development of self-control in children is facilitated.

_____ 7. Independence and self-help skills are encouraged.

Children Communication

_____ Needs improvement _____ Adequate _____ Very Good _____ Excellent

Comments:

Parents

_____ 1. Frequent contact is established and maintained with families and decisions are shared about child's care and education.

_____ 2. Parents are encouraged to observe and participate in program activities.

_____ 3. Child development knowledge, insights, and resources are shared with parents as part of regular communication.

_____ 4. Regular conferences are held with the parents and additional conferences are encouraged as needed.

Parent Communication

_____ Needs improvement _____ Adequate _____ Very Good _____ Excellent

Comments:

Staff

_____ 1. Shows respect and consideration of all employees.

_____ 2. Works cooperatively in a team approach.

_____ 3. Shows willingness to share personal talents, ideas, techniques and materials with others.

_____ 4. Solves problems by discussing them with the person or persons involved as soon as it is possible.

_____ 5. Professionally accepts suggestions and constructive criticism from other staff members.

_____ 6. Communicates/shares feelings, opinions, ideas clearly and directly with staff members.

_____ 7. Listens while other staff members speak, and is considerate of differences.

_____ 8. Participates in staff meetings, in-service training programs and center activities.

Interaction with Staff

_____ Needs improvement _____ Adequate _____ Very Good _____ Excellent

Comments:

Health and Safety

_____ 1. Children will be supervised at all times.

_____ 2. Toys, cribs and cots are to be sanitized and washed according to health policy guidelines.

_____ 3. Laundry is done according to schedule and need; including bibs, sheets, towels, washcloths, paint shirts, etc.

_____ 4. Responsibility is assumed for arrangement, care and upkeep of the program.

Health and Safety

_____ Needs improvement _____ Adequate _____ Very Good _____ Excellent

Other Requirements

_____ 1. Annual in-service training is completed within the licensing year.

_____ 2. A current First Aid and CPR certificate is maintained.

_____ 3. Completes a weekly lesson plan and submits to the Program Administrator weekly.

_____ 4. Performs other duties as required by Program Administrator.

Other Requirements

_____ Needs improvement _____ Adequate _____ Very Good _____ Excellent

Comments:

Overall Rating

_____ Needs improvement _____ Adequate _____ Very Good _____ Excellent

Administrator's Comments

_____

_____

_____

_____

_____

_____

Employee's Comments

_____

_____

_____

_____

_____

_____

Future Objectives

_____

_____

_____

_____

_____

_____

Admn. Signature _____ Date _____

Employee Signature _____ Date _____

Name _____ Position _____

	Needs Work	Satisfactory	Good	Excellent	Comments
1. Attitude toward:					
Children	_____	_____	_____	_____	_____
Parents	_____	_____	_____	_____	_____
Other Staff	_____	_____	_____	_____	_____
Interns	_____	_____	_____	_____	_____
Volunteers	_____	_____	_____	_____	_____
Program	_____	_____	_____	_____	_____
Director	_____	_____	_____	_____	_____
2. Ability to work with others	_____	_____		_____	_____
3. Responsibility when not supervised					
Takes responsibility	_____	_____	_____	_____	_____
4. Adaptability:					
Changing hours	_____	_____	_____	_____	_____
Working extra hours	_____	_____	_____	_____	_____
Helping with other groups	_____	_____	_____	_____	_____
Profits from constructive criticism	_____	_____	_____	_____	_____
5. Performance:					
Work habits	_____	_____	_____	_____	_____
Daily planning and follow-up	_____	_____	_____	_____	_____
Handling of behavior problems	_____	_____	_____	_____	_____
Outdoor supervision	_____	_____	_____	_____	_____
Meal supervision	_____	_____	_____	_____	_____
Toileting supervision	_____	_____	_____	_____	_____
Resting supervision	_____	_____	_____	_____	_____
Follows program policy	_____	_____	_____	_____	_____

	Needs Work	Satisfactory	Good	Excellent	Comments
6. Self-Development:					
Willingness to attend conferences and courses	_____	_____	_____	_____	_____
Ability to accept and use training	_____	_____	_____	_____	_____
Willingness to change	_____	_____	_____	_____	_____
Comprehension of child care	_____	_____	_____	_____	_____
Understanding of age levels	_____	_____	_____	_____	_____
7. Attendance	_____	_____	_____	_____	_____
8. Punctuality	_____	_____	_____	_____	_____
9. Appearance:					
Good grooming	_____	_____	_____	_____	_____
Cleanliness	_____	_____	_____	_____	_____
Voice and speech	_____	_____	_____	_____	_____

Staff Performance Review

Supervisors, please comment below:

Specific strengths of staff person:

_____

_____

_____

Specific limitations of staff person:

_____

_____

_____

Goals, recommendations, areas of improvement for staff person:

_____

_____

_____

Response by staff person:

_____

_____

_____

_____

_____

I have read/discussed and understand the items on this review.

Staff Signature _____

Today's date _____ Date of next evaluation _____

Supervisor _____ Director _____

© Early Childhood Directors Association (ECDA) 450 North Syndicate, Suite 5, St. Paul, MN 55104

Name _____ Position _____

Directions: Information about your performance over the past year will be collected in at least 2 ways.
1) Self-evaluation—Please indicate the number of the rating which most accurately describes how you have carried out each of the items listed below throughout the past year. The ratings are:

5 = Outstanding
4 = Exceeds Job Standards
3 = Fully Meets Job Standard
2 = Progressing/Marginal
1 = Unsatisfactory

2) Supervisor Evaluation - Your supervisor will rate how you have carried out each of the items throughout the past year. The responses from the self-evaluation and supervisor will be combined on to a single form. The information will then become the basis of discussion about current performance and direction for further development.

Interaction with Children

Self   Supervisor

_____ _____   1.   Communicates with children at eye-level (e.g., sitting on the floor, bending down, sitting at the table).
_____ _____   2.   Uses conversation with children at play and meal times.
_____ _____   3.   Nurtures the children with hugs, laughs and appropriate touches.
_____ _____   4.   Participates in children's play when appropriate.
_____ _____   5.   Uses problem solving strategies in helping children deal with situations.
_____ _____   6.   Offers children opportunities for decision making and choices.
_____ _____   7.   Follows through consistently with behavior guidance techniques.
_____ _____   8.   Uses positive words when giving directions (do's rather than don'ts).

_____ _____   9.   Shows empathy and acceptance of children's feelings.
_____ _____   10. Assists children in using appropriate language to communicate.
_____ _____   11. Demonstrates awareness of total group even when dealing with an individual child or small group.
_____ _____   12. Demonstrates knowledge about growth and development of young children.
_____ _____   13. Demonstrates knowledge about the meaning of specific activities for children.

Interaction with parents

Self   Supervisor

_____ _____   1.   Is supportive of parents in the care and development of their child.
_____ _____   2.   Demonstrates an understanding and tolerance that situations cannot always be handled at home as they are in the program.
_____ _____   3.   Keeps parents informed of child's daily activities and progress.
_____ _____   4.   Follows through on requests made by parents regarding the care of their child.
_____ _____   5.   Talks with parents comfortably.
_____ _____   6.   Demonstrates tact, compassion, and empathetic concern for parents.

Interaction with Staff

Self   Supervisor

_____ _____ 1. Makes a real effort to become involved in the program.
_____ _____ 2. Accepts share of responsibility and tasks assigned.
_____ _____ 3. Respects the rights and teaching techniques of others on the staff.
_____ _____ 4. Demonstrates willingness to consider new ideas.
_____ _____ 5. Shows willingness to share personal talents, ideas, techniques. and materials with others.
_____ _____ 6. Accepts suggestions and constructive criticism from other staff members gracefully.
_____ _____ 7. Communicates/shares feelings, opinions and ideas clearly and directly with all staff members.
_____ _____ 8. Listens while other staff members speak, is considerate of differences.
_____ _____ 9. Participates in discussions during staff meetings.
_____ _____ 10. Works cooperatively with other staff members.

Personal Responsibilities

Self   Supervisor

_____ _____ 1. Speaks clearly and distinctly.
_____ _____ 2. Smiles and shows enjoyment often.
_____ _____ 3. Is dependable and energetic.
_____ _____ 4. Is able to objectively evaluate self.
_____ _____ 5. Can follow directions.
_____ _____ 6. Displays a generally positive attitude towards work.
_____ _____ 7. Demonstrates professional growth through participation in inservice program.
_____ _____ 8. Is enthusiastic and excited about working with young children.
_____ _____ 9. Has a sense of humor.

Strengths:

Possible areas for growth:

Area of concentration for professional growth during 19 _____

Staff person's signature _____

Director's signature _____

Date _____

Please rank yourself using the following criteria:

5 = Outstanding:	performance is so outstanding that it approximates the maximum that can be expected.
4 = Superior:	performance consistently exceeds job requirements.
3 = Fully Competent:	performance consistently meets all job requirements.
2 = Developing Competence:	performance is below the level of good performance, but improvements are being seen.
1 = Needs Improvement:	performance is well below the minimum level.

INTERPERSONAL SKILLS – Children

Admin. Staff

_____ _____ Interacts with children to develop their self esteem
- [ ] greets children individually upon arrival
- [ ] calls children by name
- [ ] bends over, stoops down or sits to maintain eye contact
- [ ] speaks to individual children often
- [ ] encourages independence in children by asking for their assistance in tasks; lets them complete tasks themeselves
- [ ] verbally interacts with individual children during routines
- [ ] listens to children

_____ _____ Develops meaningful relationships with children
- [ ] shows respect, consideration, and warmth
- [ ] respects individual needs of children
- [ ] allows as much time as possible to listen to each child
- [ ] plans for skills and interests of individual children

_____ _____ Sensitive to individual child's needs
- [ ] treats all races, religions and cultures equally
- [ ] provides children of both sexes with equal opportunities
- [ ] take part in all activities
- [ ] responds to children's verbal and non-verbal indications of needs or requests

_____ _____ Interacts with group
- [ ] smiles
- [ ] moves to children to talk rather than calling from a distance
- [ ] uses low, calm voice during interactions

Interpersonal Skills

Admin. Staff

_____ _____ Maintains a positive relationship with staff members
☐ shows sensitivity toward staff's individual needs
☐ willing to work with and for others
☐ carries own share of responsibilities

_____ _____ Works cooperatively in a team approach
☐ shares ideas (staff meetings, curriculum planning, etc.)
☐ can give and accept constructive suggestions
☐ shares responsibilities in a team setting
☐ follows through on commitments

Interpersonal Skills – Parents

_____ _____ Communicates with parents effectively in a friendly manner
☐ frequently
☐ clearly

_____ _____ Communicates progress of children to parents
☐ informally but regularly
☐ formal conferences

Curriculum

_____ _____ Prepares and carries out daily activities that are designed for the developmental level and individual needs of the children in assigned group
☐ turns in weekly planning form
☐ daily program includes a balance of:
☐ quiet and active activities
☐ child-initiated and teacher directed activities
☐ fine motor and gross motor activities
☐ regularly contains a variety of activities that includes:

☐ sensory activities	☐ field trips
☐ art	☐ cooking
☐ science	☐ group activities
☐ music	☐ child created stories
☐ large motor	☐ dramatic play
☐ small motor	☐ language development
☐ movement	☐ telling/reading stories
☐ math readiness	

☐ incorporates a variety of media in plans
☐ activities are set up in a way to motivate children to explore and learn through their play
☐ materials are set up for the children ahead of time to avoid a waiting period

Admin. Staff

_____ _____ Curriculum reflects creativity and new ideas
☐ individual interests of the children are incorporated in curriculum
☐ a variety of resources are used in planning curriculum

_____ _____ Recognizes needs of children and plans activities so that children will succeed
☐ insures that there is enough for children to do at all times
☐ flexible, adaptable to differing situations
☐ plans for the most and least skilled children

Classroom Environment

_____ _____ Classroom is maintained in an attractive manner
☐ classroom appears stimulating and ordered
☐ children's art work is displayed
☐ shares in daily responsibilities for maintaining the environment
☐ takes initiative in setting up new materials in the room
☐ materials are rotated on a regular basis
☐ the following interest areas are set up:
☐ sand and water play   ☐ table toys
☐ blocks   ☐ library area
☐ variety of props
☐ dramatic play

_____ _____ Safety of the children is demonstrated in the environment
☐ no broken equipment
☐ no open runways
☐ toys and containers for toys are in repair
☐ teacher models, teaches respect of materials

Health and Safety

_____ _____ Monitors the whereabouts of children at all times
☐ insures the safe arrival and departure of the children
☐ is aware of who is picking up children at all times
☐ maintains supervision by sight and sound
☐ monitors when children use the bathroom, and are in the hall

_____ _____ Encourages healthy habits in the children
☐ includes nutrition in regular lesson plans
☐ encourages children to brush teeth after eating
☐ has children wash hands before eating, after using the toilet and after blowing their nose

© Early Childhood Directors Association (ECDA) 450 North Syndicate, Suite 5, St. Paul, MN 55104

Guidance and discipline

Admin. Staff

_____ _____ Maintains order during smooth transitions
  ☐ prepares ahead for transitions
  ☐ controls group even when dealing with individual child

_____ _____ Enforces limits in consistent and fair manner
  ☐ limits have been explained clearly to each child
  ☐ tries to avoid most discipline problems by being organized and prepared

_____ _____ Creates an environment that leads children to self-control
  ☐ helps children accept responsibility for their own behavior
  ☐ activities are designed to foster independence and responsibility
  ☐ redirects, distracts or channels disruptive play into acceptable outlets
  ☐ guides children in effective ways of settling disputes
  ☐ encourages children to talk about their feelings and ideas rather than use physical force
  ☐ tells children what they can do, giving alternatives
  ☐ models behavior expected of the children

Professionalism

_____ _____ Is reliable, punctual and regular in attendance
  ☐ takes appropriate amount of time on breaks
  ☐ notifies director well in advance of absence from the program

_____ _____ Is professional in job
  ☐ maintains confidentiality of child and family information
  ☐ participates in staff meetings
  ☐ maintains a program of professional growth in in-service training
  ☐ demonstrates an understanding of the program's policies and philosophies

_____ _____ Is professional with children
  ☐ is tolerant and considerate of differences in children and adults
  ☐ aware of own negative feelings aroused by an individual child and can recognize, verbalize and handle these feelings in appropriate ways
  ☐ remains calm and uses good judgement in tense situations
  ☐ maintains a sense of humor with children and adults

Teacher completes the following:

What are the goals that you have set for the children in your care?

_____

_____

_____

How do you incorporate these goals in to your daily lesson plans, and your interaction with the children?

_____

_____

_____

In what areas do you feel you are most successful in your job?

_____

_____

_____

In what areas would you like to concentrate on improving in the next six months? How can the director help you in these areas?

_____

_____

Date _____

Employee Signature _____

Evaluation _____

© Early Childhood Directors Association (ECDA) 450 North Syndicate, Suite 5, St. Paul, MN 55104

Name _____

Job Title _____

Date _____

Length of time in this position _____

The first part of this evaluation is a self-evaluation. The purpose is to point out different areas of importance in the program, and for the individual staff member to see where they are meeting the needs in these areas. These will be discussed during the oral evaluation. Be as honest as possible; the goal is to acknowledge strengths and to work on areas of need.

To maintain a safe, healthy, interesting and enjoyable learning environment, one that encourages exploration and learning by the children.

1.   I encourage children to follow common safety practices when I . . .

_____

_____

2.   I stop and redirect unsafe child behavior by. . .

_____

_____

3.   1 encourage children to follow common health and nutrition practices by . . .

_____

_____

4.   I arrange equipment and materials so that children can make choices easily and independently by . . .

_____

_____

5.   I help develop separate activity areas and places for the children by . . .

_____

_____

© Early Childhood Directors Association (ECDA) 450 North Syndicate, Suite 5, St. Paul, MN 55104

To advance physical and intellectual competence.

1.   I provide opportunities for children to move their bodies in a variety of ways by . . .

_____

_____

2.   I interact with children in ways that encourage them to think and solve problems when I . . .

_____

_____

3.   I interact with children in ways that encourage them to communicate their thoughts and feelings verbally. An example is . . .

_____

_____

4.   I use books and stories with children to motivate listening and speaking. An example is . . .

_____

_____

5.   I accept children's creative products without placing a value judgement on them. When a child shows me his/her work I say. . .

_____

_____

6.   I arrange art materials for the children to explore on their own by. . .

_____

_____

To support social and emotional development and provide positive guidance.

1.   I accept every child as a worthy human being and let him or her know this with these nonverbal cues:

_____

_____

2.   I help children to accept and appreciate themselves and each other by. . .

_____

_____

3.   I help, but not pressure, the shy child to interact with others by. . .

_____

_____

4.   I help the children respect the rights and understand the feelings of others by. . .

_____

_____

5.   Some positive guidance methods I use to help children control their negative behavior are . . .

_____

_____

To establish positive and productive relationships with families.

1.   I communicate with parents when . . .

_____

_____

2.   I communicate with parents by . . .

_____

_____

To maintain a commitment to professionalism.

1.   I have taken these opportunities to improve my professional growth. . .

_____

_____

2.   I treat information about children and families confidentially by . . .

_____

_____

Staff Name _____

Date _____

Director's Signature _____

Work Habits

• Do I arrive at work with a cheerful positive attitude? _____

• Have I been conscientious in my attendance? _____

• Do I assume responsibility for arrangement, care and upkeep of our program? _____

• Am I a staff member that can be depended upon for pitching in when needed? _____

Relationships and Communication with Staff

• Do I display tact, courtesy and consideration to other staff? _____

• Do I accept suggestions and constructive criticisms from other staff members gracefully? _____

• Have I remained flexible in my relationships with other staff? _____

• Have I been able to retain my composure in tense situations? _____

• Have I avoided indulging in gossip about other staff members? _____

• Do I show willingness to share personal talents with my peers? _____

• Do I work cooperatively in a team approach? _____

• Do I keep my voice low so I am not heard over the children's voices? _____

• Am I friendly with other staff but careful not to take time from children by visiting? _____

With Children

• Do I use a soft, gentle, affirming voice when speaking to the children? _____

• Do I help a child feel at home wanted and loved? _____

• Am I sensitive to individual children their interests and needs? _____

• Do I have a wholesome sense of humor with children? _____

• Am I aware of my own negative or positive feelings aroused by other adults with whom I work? _____

With Parents

• Have I developed a warm relationship with the parents of the children? _____

• Do I show respect and consideration for each parent and listen to their ideas, feelings and concerns? _____

Teaching Skills

• Do I make interesting and appropriate contributions to curriculum planning? _____

• Do I make use of both in-program and outside resources in order to expand and enrich my program ideas?_____

• Do I anticipate materials needed for planned projects so everything is ready when I need it? _____

• Have I been able to retain an overview of the class situation? _____

• Is my voice well-modulated and pleasant? _____

• Am I able to hold the children's attention during group activities? _____

• Can I improvise in class when the need arises? _____

• Am I able to be flexible in my lesson plans in order to meet the needs of the children? _____

Understanding our program

• Do I understand the overall activities of our program? _____

• Have I displayed a willingness to participate in pertinent program activities outside of regular hours? _____

• Do I feel comfortable giving feedback and input into the operation of the program? _____

• Do I feel loyalty to the program? _____

• Have I carried positive and professional attitudes about the school into my community activities? _____

Please add your comments to the following questions:

1. Name specific areas you feel you need to develop further in your teaching: _____

_____

2. Name specific areas in which you feel most adequate and find the most satisfying:

_____

3. I have _____ hours of classes/workshops since the last licensing. I plan to take a class/workshop

on _____

Evaluator comments _____

_____

© Early Childhood Directors Association (ECDA) 450 North Syndicate, Suite 5, St. Paul, MN 55104

Self-Evaluation of a Team

Directions: Think about how your fellow group members normally behave toward you. In the spaces in front of the items below, place the letter that corresponds to your perceptions of their behavior.

A - They can **always** be counted on to behave.this way

T - **Typically** I would expect them to behave this way

U - I would **usually** expect them to behave this way

S - They would **seldom** behave this way

R - They would **rarely** behave this way

N - I would **never** expect them to behave this way

I would expect my fellow group members to:

1. _____ level with me

2. _____ get the drift of what I am trying to say

3. _____ interrupt or ignore my comments

4. _____ accept me for what I am

5. _____ feel free to let me know when I "bug" them

6. _____ misconstrue things I say or do

7. _____ be interested in me

8. _____ provide an atmosphere in which I can be myself

9. _____ keep things to themselves to spare my feelings

10. _____ perceive what kind of person I really am

11. _____ include me in what's going on

12. _____ be completely frank with me

13. _____ recognize when something is bothering me

14. _____ act "judgemental" with me

15. _____ respect me, apart from my skills or status

Self-Evaluation of a Team

Directions: Rate your group on each characteristic as it is now. Use a 7 point scale, with 7 as the highest rating, and 1 as the lowest.

Climate

_____ I am treated as a human being, not as just another group member

_____ I feel close to the members of this group

_____ This group displays cooperation and teamwork

_____ Membership in this group is aiding my personal growth

_____ I have trust and confidence in the other members of this group

_____ Members of this group show supportive behavior toward each other

_____ I derive satisfaction from my membership in this group

_____ I feel psychologically close to this group

_____ I get a sense of accomplishment from my membership in this group

_____ I am being honest in responding to this evaluation

Data Flow

_____ I am willing to share information with other members of the group

_____ I feel free to discuss important personal matters with group members

Goal Formation

_____ I am orientated toward personal goals rather than toward group objectives

_____ This group uses integrative, constructive methods in problem-solving rather than a competitive approach

_____ I am able to deal promptly and well with the important problems of this group

_____ The activities of this group reflect a constructive integration of the needs and desires of its members

_____ My needs and desires are reflected in the activities of this group

Control

_____ This group has a real sense of responsibility for getting a job done

_____ I feel manipulated by the group

_____ I think that I manipulate the group

Self-Evaluation of Attitude

Name _____

In regard to my job at _____ :
                              program

1. Right now I am most content about: _____

2. The most frustrating issue right now is: _____

3. I'm glad for the change in: _____

My overall work attitude this month is:

1   2   3   4   5   6   7   8   9   10
Poor   ❤

I'd like to meet next _____ at _____
                              day   time

Additional Comments:

	yes	no
I like my hours	_____	_____
I'd like to work more	_____	_____
I'd like to work less	_____	_____
I'd be willing to fill in for someone when they're absent	_____	_____	_____ Hrs. available

Self-Evaluation of Attitude

1. What are some of the things that help make you feel satisfied or dissatisfied with your job?

_____

_____

2. Do you feel that you are part of the decision-making team? If not, how could you feel that you are?

_____

_____

3. Do you feel motivated to grow in your job and/or profession? If so, what motivates you?

_____

_____

4. How long do you plan to stay in your job? What are the factors that will contribute to that decision?

_____

_____

5. Please use other side to give me ANY feedback.

_____

_____

Self-Evaluation of Attitude

An area of this program that frustrates me is _____

_____

An area I have improved the most in is _____

_____

If I could change one thing about my job, it would be

_____

_____

How do you feel we are progressing towards achieving the program's philosophy/goals? _____

_____

_____

As teachers of young children, it is important to realize that we need interpersonal skills (understanding others) and intrapersonal skills (understanding ourselves), in addition to curriculum development and implementation, and effective teaching techniques. This exercise is designed to help us look at our ability to understand ourselves and others, and to provide some insight as to how we might solve some of the problems we have with our relationships. Be as honest as you can. No one will see this paper but you.

Have you had a problem recently with someone with whom you work? _____

How recently? _____

Briefly describe the problem _____

_____

How did you feel about the problem then? _____

_____

How do you feel about the problem now? _____

_____

Did you talk about the problem with the other person? _____

If not, why not? If yes, what was the result? _____

_____

Did you talk with someone else about the problem? _____

If not, why not? If yes, what was the result? _____

_____

Is this problem the kind that you have fairly frequently; once in awhile; or is this the first time?

_____

Now, briefly describe the person with whom you had the problem? _____

_____

_____

Stop for a few minutes and think about the problem from the viewpoint of this other person. Just think for a little while, don't write yet.

Now, describe the problem as you think s/he might describe it. _____

_____

_____

How do you think s/he felt about the problem then? _____

_____

_____

How do you think s/he feels about the problem now?

_____

_____

Did s/he talk with you about the problem? If not, why not, do you think? _____

_____

_____

Did s/he talk with anyone else about the problem? If so, why do you think s/he did this? _____

_____

_____

Now, having looked at the problem from two points of view, have your feelings about this problem changed? If so, how?

_____

_____

Pretend for a minute. If you and this other person took your problem to a third person for help, how do you think this person would describe the problem and what do you think would be suggested for a solution?

_____

_____

How would you describe yourself, generally? Please check those that apply.

_____ I am quick-tempered.

_____ I let my temper out (arguing, shouting, hitting something, etc.)

_____ I hold my temper in (get headaches or stomach aches, cry, etc.)

_____ I hold grudges.

_____ I deal with problems directly.

_____ I take care of myself.

_____ I talk with others about my anger, but not to those with whom I am angry.

_____ I am fearful and anxious about confrontation with others. I want others to take care of problems and leave me alone.

_____ I am fair-minded.

_____ I generally trust people.

_____ I am often critical.

_____ I don't trust many people.

_____ I am easy going, quite friendly.

_____ I am uptight a lot and not very friendly.

_____ Mostly, I just want to complain, get someone to listen to me.

_____ I don't want anything done about the problem.

_____ When I complain I want something done, right away!

_____ When I complain about anything, I try to offer a solution to the problem.

_____ I want people to accept me as I am. I don't want to have to change myself or my attitudes.

_____ I'm willing to change some things, if others will change, too.

Now, look at the things you have checked and think about what they mean to you. Put a check to the right of the items you don't like very much, and that you think you could change.

How many did you check on the left? _____

How many on the right? _____

Is there one particular trait that causes problems with others? _____

If so, why does it cause trouble?_____

_____

Is there any one thing that others do that particularly annoys you? _____

If so, why does it bother you? _____

_____

Do you think these two behaviors you've just thought about can be helped with some training, some thinking and self-discipline, discussion groups, other ideas? _____

What would help and why? _____

_____

_____

_____

How important are good staff relationships to you? Why? _____

_____

_____

How important do you think they are to those with whom you work? _____

Why?_____

_____

_____

Now, tell yourself three positive things about yourself that you can do to make your work place a good place to be for everyone._____

_____

_____

Wow! That's wonderful. Keep up the good work!

© Early Childhood Directors Association (ECDA) 450 North Syndicate, Suite 5, St. Paul, MN 55104   PERFORMANCE APPRAISAL   167

Lesson Evaluation Sheet

Teacher _____ Date _____

Lesson Plan _____ Age Group _____

Rating key: 4 = Outstanding; 3 = Good; 2 = Satisfactory; 1 = Needs Improvement

	Rating	Comments
Introduction & Motivation		
Objectives (clarity of purpose)		
Use of materials & equipment		
Presentation		
Control & discipline		
Conclusion & follow-up		
Time element		
Number of children participating		

The following are good points regarding your lesson:

_____

_____

I feel that you need to improve upon the following:

_____

_____

Suggestions:

_____

_____

Avg. rating [ ] Teacher's signature _____

Observer's signature _____

Dear Staff:

The importance of quality administration is as important as the quality of all our staff. We ask that you take some time to fill out the survey below.

There are five areas of concentration. If there are additional comments, please use back of this form. Thank you for your time. Your signature is optional.

S=strong   A=average   NI=needs improvement

Communication

_____ dispensing of information

_____ listening skills

_____ approachability

_____ voice

_____ giving and accepting criticism

Supervision

_____ evaluating

_____ delegating responsibilities

_____ follow through

Staff

_____ hiring/firing procedures

_____ expectations of staff... clear and concise

_____ team building approach

_____ sensitivity to staff's personal needs

_____ supports and encourages staff

_____ role models for staff

Time management

_____ planning

_____ developing program goals

_____ availability

_____ reliability

Professional

_____ dress

_____ language

_____ parent/child relations

_____ shows enthusiasm and interest in job

Continued

Please indicate the extent to which you feel the director is providing for your needs in the following areas:

Need	Enough	Need More	Less	Different
1. Material supplies				
2. Food supplies				
3. Equipment				
4. Curriculum planning				
5. Field trips				
6. Consultation about individual children				
7. Help with children who are difficult				
8. Communication with parents (conferences)				
9. In-service training				
10. Effective staff meetings				
11. Consultation about staff relations				
12. Consultation about teaching performance				
13. Information about salary and benefits				
14. Information about job responsibilities				
15. Information about scheduling of events				
16. Involvement in development of our program				
17. Updating on matters which affect our program				
18. Realistic expectations (time, responsibilities etc)				

Please list suggestions for improvement of our program, working conditions, and the director's performance.

How could the director be more help to you?

_____

_____

How would you like your relationship to the director to change?

_____

_____

Do you have other needs which are not being met?

_____

_____

Thank you for taking time to thoughtfully consider these areas - your input is valuable and necessary in order to continue to offer a quality program for parents and children, and a positive working environment for staff. Please use the back of page for any additional comments.

Workshop Evaluation

Please complete and return to the office.   Date_____

How did you like the staff workshop day? _____

_____

What did you like about the day? _____

_____

What would you change about the day? _____

_____

Was the time frame comfortable for you?

A.M. _____

P.M. _____

Did you feel the speakers were useful to you?

A.M. _____

P.M. _____

Did you feel that the speakers were well prepared?

A.M. _____

P.M. _____

In what way was the information useful to you?

A.M. _____

P.M. _____

What information did you feel was not useful to you?

A.M. _____

P.M. _____

Did you feel that the speakers respected our program?

A.M. _____

P.M. _____

If you need additional space, please use the back.

Thank you for taking the time to complete this evaluation.

Curriculum

This section includes forms that may assist staff in developing their daily program of activities for children of various ages.

Infant Daily Report (Form 1)

Name_____ Change in phone number for today _____

Change in emergency contact person_____Phone _____

Time of Arrival: _____

Baby Seems
_____ Active as usual
_____ A bit fussy
_____ Not acting as usual_____
_____

Baby Slept
_____ Soundly
_____ Did not sleep well
_____ Time baby woke up

Baby Ate
_____ Breakfast before coming
_____ Bottle only before coming
_____ Food only before coming
_____ Nothing before coming
_____ Time

Bottles
_____ oz. at _____
_____ oz. at _____
_____ oz. at _____

Bowel Movements
_____ Hard _____
_____ Soft _____
_____ Normal _____
_____ Loose _____
_____ Diarrhea _____

Medication
Dosage _____
Given by _____

Accidents today:
_____

Special Instructions
_____ Diet change
_____ Activities to avoid
_____ Medication

Accident at home?
Bodily location _____
Type _____

Sleeping
_____ to _____
_____ to _____
_____ to _____
_____ to _____

Needs
_____ Diapers
_____ Bottom wipes
_____ Bottle liners
_____ Jar food
_____ Cereal
_____ Formula
_____ Extra clothes
_____ Diaper ointment

Younger:
Cereal or Meat
_____ at _____
_____ at _____
Fruit
_____ at _____
_____ at _____
Vegetables
_____ at _____
_____ at _____

Solid Food
Older:
Breakfast
_____ Ate good portion
_____ Ate none
_____ Ate all
Lunch
_____ Ate good portion
_____ Ate none
_____ Ate all
Snack: _____

© Early Childhood Directors Association (ECDA) 450 North Syndicate, Suite 5, St. Paul, MN 55104

Infant Daily Report (Form 2)

Name _____ Date _____ Time _____

Who will drop off? _____ Time _____

Who will pick up? _____ Time _____

Developmental

    Comforting _____

    Favorite Toy _____

    Special Activities _____

Sleeping

    Special ways to help the infant go to sleep _____

_____

    Stomach/Back/Side _____

    Present sleeping schedule _____

    Night time _____

    AM _____

    PM _____

    _____ Pacifier

    _____ Special Blanket

    _____ Special Toy

Feeding

    Bottle/Nursing _____

    Bottle Schedule _____

Burping _____

Eating Schedule

    _____ Breakfast _____ Lunch _____ Snacks

Special ways of feeding _____

    Fast/Slow _____

Toileting

    BM _____ How Frequently _____ Appearance _____ Diaper Rash _____

Misc.

Any other information _____

_____

174 FORMS KIT

Infant Daily Report (Form 3)

_____'s night at home

When did your baby:

      Wake up _____

      Last ate _____

      How much _____

How did your baby sleep? _____

Has any medication been given? _____ How much _____ What time _____

Any medication needed _____ How much _____ What time _____

Any information you would like us to know for the day?

_____

_____

Feeding		Napping
Time	Ounces	_____ to _____
_____	_____	_____ to _____
_____	_____	_____ to _____
_____	_____	_____ to _____
_____	_____	
_____	_____	**Diapering**
_____	_____	Time Type*
_____	_____	_____ _____

Food

Breakfast

_____

Lunch

_____

Diapering entries:

Time	Type*
_____	_____
_____	_____
_____	_____
_____	_____
_____	_____
_____	_____
_____	_____

I need:

_____ Tylenol

_____ Pediacare

_____ Formula

_____ Baby Food

_____ Clothes

_____ Other

*

F=Firm

L=Loose

W=Wet

N=Normal

Miscellaneous Information _____

_____

Age Group: Toddler

Daily Schedule	Objectives	Activities	Methods
7:00 AM - 8:45 AM Arrival & Creative Play (Diapering/toileting occurs during this time as needed)	Health check, parent contact. Open free-play, child chooses activities he/she feels comfortable doing. Social interaction, sharing, develop independence, cognitive and small muscle development, eye hand coordination and listening skills.	Materials include books, tapes & records, puzzles, unit blocks, small manipulatives, crayons, markers, paper, puppets, stringing beads, playdough.	Children move freely in this area, teacher helping when needed, reading stories and doing musical activities in small groups. Also games and finger plays. Another teacher is in the entrance area greeting children and parents.
8:00 - 8:30 AM Breakfast	Nutrition, form good eating habits, develop good table manners.	Children have their own cereal which is provided by parents. Milk is provided by the center. When the child is finished, he/she rejoins the group.	One teacher is at the table with children, assisting when needed. Bibs are provided by the center.
8:45 - 8:55 AM Clean up	Learn to follow direction, how to work together, respect for others and their property, and general cooperation skills.	Teacher rings a bell and sometimes a song is sung as each child puts equipment away.	Child is encouraged to help a friend when he/she is finished in one area.
9:00 -9:10 AM (Diapering/toileting and handwashing)	Learn good health habits, how to follow directions and to develop independence in personal hygiene.	One teacher assists with children who need diapering and the other teacher assists those going to the toilet.	There are ___ bathrooms containing a total of ___ sinks and ___ toilets and ___ changing table. No child must wait too long for his/her turn.
9:10 - 9:30 Snack time	A nutritious snack is served. Table manners, taking turns, cleaning up together.	Snacks are planned for the month, using a balance of the 4 basic food groups, keeping nutrition in mind.	The snack is prepared during the resting period. Teachers sit with children for all meals.
9:30 -10:00 Small Group	Cognitive and language activities such as concepts of color, object identification, following directions.	Books, tapes, flannel board, chalk board, small blocks, musical instruments, records.	Mostly teacher directed activities, each child having time for self expression.

Continued

Age Group: Toddler

Daily Schedule	Objectives	Activities	Methods
10:00 - 10:30 AM Large Group	Art/Sensory activities to allow creativity and expression. Also cognitive and small muscle development, follow directions.	Hand art work, crayons, finger paint, markers, pasting, cooking, sand and water play, rice play.	New experiences that can be messy and fun and allow for language stimulation and an opportunity for labeling.
10:30 - 10:40 AM Diapering/Toileting/ Handwashing	See above		
10:45 - 11:15 AM Outdoor Play	Gross motor and large muscle. Also learning to dress; hat, jacket, mittens, boots.	Children are free to choose climber swings, slide, see-saw, balls, sand box, and many riding toys.	Fenced area allows children to move around freely and practice newly acquired skills.
11:20 - 11:45 AM Lunch	Develop table manners, learn good nutrition, taking turns, learn to clean up after themselves.	Each child bring his/her own lunch box (brought from home) to the table. Teacher sits with group and helps when needed.	Unfinished items are returned to the lunch box so that parents are aware of what was eaten.
11:45 - 12:15 PM Story time	Quiet time in preparation for rest.	Puppets, books, tapes, rocking chair.	Some times this period is teacher directed and other times child can choose a quiet activity and help set up the cots.
12:15 - 12:30 PM Diapering/Toileting/ Handwashing	See above		
Rest Time	Children help prepare cots, and teachers help child relax in preparation for sleep.	Cots, bags containing blanket, rest toy are brought from closet and set up in rooms. Soft music is played on tape player.	Learn the importance of resting and how we are happier and healthier when well rested. Teacher will wake up those children who are still resting at parents request.
2:45 - 3:00 PM Diapering/Toileting/ Handwashing Put away cots	See above		

Continued

Daily Schedule	Objectives	Activities	Methods
3:00 - 3:20 PM Snack time	See morning snack time		
3:25 - 3:50 PM Creative Playtime	Dramatic play offers opportunity to act out daily activities from home; making dinner, going to work, etc. Block building is another opportunity to make homes, garages, and other familiar things in their environment.	Child free to choose kitchen, home living center, waffle blocks, soft blocks, and junior climber.	Teachers assist in the areas needed.
3:50 - 4:00 PM Diapering/Toileting/ Handwashing			
4:05 - 4:35 PM Outdoor Play	See 10:45 AM Outdoor Play		
4:45 - 5:30 PM Large Group	Group gathers in transition room for creative play and to await parents arrival.	Equipment includes books, tapes, playdough, puzzles, unit blocks, small manipulatives, crayons, rocking boat, bead rack.	Children are free to choose activity. There are large windows in this room to allow child to watch for parents arrival.

© Early Childhood Directors Association (ECDA) 450 North Syndicate, Suite 5, St. Paul, MN 55104

Toddler Weekly Form

For the week of _____

_____'s Parent-Teacher Exchange

Day	Breakfast	Total Hours Slept	Behavior Changes	Parent's Comments/Instructions	Diaper Changes	Ate Well	Slept at Nap	Teacher Comments
M	Yes / No		Yes / No		Yes / No	Well / OK / Poorly	Yes / No	
T	Yes / No		Yes / No		Yes / No	Well / OK / Poorly	Yes / No	
W	Yes / No		Yes / No		Yes / No	Well / OK / Poorly	Yes / No	
Th	Yes / No		Yes / No		Yes / No	Well / OK / Poorly	Yes / No	
F	Yes / No		Yes / No		Yes / No	Well / OK / Poorly	Yes / No	

Toddler Daily Note

Changes in phone number or emergency contact _____ Child _____

At home _____

Seemed:
_____ active as usual
_____ a bit fussy
_____ not acting as usual

Slept:
_____ soundly
_____ did not sleep well
_____ time child woke up _____

Ate:
_____ breakfast before coming
_____ nothing before coming
_____ time child last ate _____

Accident at home?
Bodily location _____
Type _____

Special Instructions:
Diet changes _____
Activities to avoid _____
Medication _____

Approximate departure time _____

At the center
Disposition:
_____ shared with others
_____ shows curiosity and interest in surroundings
_____ finds own play area or activity
_____ happy and played well
_____ enjoyed activities today
_____ needed more attention today
_____ tired
_____ did not participate much today
_____ _____

Self-help
_____ helped put toys away
_____ washed own face and hands
_____ tried to pull up own pants after changing
_____ used potty without help
_____ used potty with help

Eating

	Breakfast	Lunch	Snack
Protein			
Fruit			
Vegetable			
Bread/Cereal			
Dairy			
Juice			
Other			

Comments
_____
_____

Today I
_____ slept
_____ rested quietly
_____ was restless

Diapering and Potty

Time	D or P	Consistency	Comments

Hard, Normal, Soft, Loose, Diarrhea

Needs
_____ Diapers
_____ Bottom wipes
_____ Bottom ointment
_____ Extra clothes
_____ other _____

Toddler Potty Chart

Codes

Codes	As child comes into b.r. / What child does in b.r.	W = Wet BM = Soiled D = Dry > as child comes into b.r.	O = Did not sit on potty N= Sat but no results W= Wet on potty B.M. = Had B.M. on potty > What child did in b.r.

Names	Health O.K.	Morning 7:30 - 11:15		Drink	Lunch Time 11:15 - 12:30		Teeth	After Naps 1:00 - 3:00		Drink	Afternoon 3:15 - 5:30		Drink

Schedule	Objectives	Procedures
6:30 - 8:45 AM Arrival: Self-interest time	To make each child feel welcome and comfortable. To greet each parent and take a few minutes to discuss any questions or concerns. To offer a variety of activities to engage children's interests.	Greet each child and parent with a cheerful hello or good morning. Do a quick check for an unhealthy child. Have assorted activities available and participate with the children.
8:45 - 9:00 AM Clean-up and preparation for breakfast	To insure a clean and healthy environment. To promote good health habits.	Each child cleans up their own area and gets an opportunity to assist in setting up for breakfast. Each child washes hands and uses bathroom facilities if necessary.
9:00 - 9:30 AM Breakfast	To promote good eating habits and to provide an opportunity for social interaction.	Eat family style by sitting together and passing food around, encouraging children to serve themselves and to use polite eating habits.
9:30 - 10:00 AM Group Time	To promote social interaction within a structured group situation.	Start off each morning with "carpet time," giving each a chance to express feelings or events of the day. Then the teacher selects various activities to coincide with weekly theme, e.g. music, circle games, calendar, weather, helpers, etc.
10:00 - 10:45 AM Small Group Activities	To encourage communication and participation. To increase skill levels and knowledge. To develop socialization skills.	Teacher provides a variety of art activities, games, or special activities.
10:45 - 11:00 AM Toileting	To develop good health habits.	Each child washes hands and uses bathroom facilities.
11:00 - 11:45 AM Outdoor play; Large muscle time.	To allow for outdoor play (weather permitting). To develop cooperation, self-reliance, and creative expression. For relaxation and enjoyment.	Outdoors: games, walks, freeplay, swings, sandbox, etc. Large muscle room: games, special exercise activities, free play, climber, etc.

Continued

Schedule	Objectives	Procedures
11:45 - 12:00 PM Preparation for lunch	To insure a clear and healthy environment. To promote good health and eating habits.	Each child washes hands and uses bathroom facilities if necessary.
12:00 - 12:30 PM Lunch	To promote good eating habits and to provide an opportunity for social interaction.	Eat family style by sitting together and passing food around, encouraging children to serve themselves and to use polite eating habits.
12:30 - 1:30 PM Quiet Time	To provide a healthful rest and time to oneself.	Each child plays quietly by him/herself for the first half, then plays quietly with one or two other friends. Each child uses bathroom facilities if needed.
1:30 - 2:30 PM Small Group Activities	To encourage communication and participation. To increase knowledge. To develop socialization skills.	Teacher provides a variety of art activities, games, or special activities.
2:30 - 3:15 PM Special Activities & Self Interest	To introduce a variety of activities for learning as well as pleasure.	Read a story. Recite fingerplays. Sing songs. Listen to records. Puppet plays. Dramatic Play area. Art projects, etc.
3:15 - 3:45 PM Toileting, snack and/or self-interest time	To promote good eating habits. To offer a variety of activities and make sure each child is constructively occupied.	Child decides when they want snack. Snack is prepared and ready. If not eating snack, child can choose own activity. Teacher participates with children. Each child washes hands and uses bathroom facilities if necessary.
3:45 - 4:30 PM Outdoor play; Large muscle time	Same as morning.	Same as morning.
4:30 - 6:00 PM Departure; self-interest time	To prepare children to go home and say their good-byes.	Make sure everyone has all their belongings. Say good-bye until the next day.

© Early Childhood Directors Association (ECDA) 450 North Syndicate, Suite 5, St. Paul, MN 55104

Weekly Planning Form (Form1)

Week of _____ Special Focus/Theme _____

Changes to the environment	Housekeeping	Art	Sensory
	Blocks	Manipulatives	Books and Quiet

	Monday	**Tuesday**	**Wednesday**	**Thursday**	**Friday**
Group Time • Songs • Stories • Games Outdoor or Large Muscle					

Weekly Planning Form (Form 2)

Teacher _____ Time Span _____ Week of _____

Area	Monday	Tuesday	Wednesday	Thursday	Friday
Creative Open-Ended Art Activities					
Building Imaginative Play					
Dramatic Play					
Math/Science Social Studies Exploration					
Puzzles/ Table Games					
Literature/ Language					
Active Indoor/ Outdoor Activities					
Health, Safety Self-Help Skills					
Fine Arts					
Special Events					

Weekly Planning Form (Form 3)

Teacher: _____

Class: _____

Weekly Theme: _____

Week of: _____

Concepts

Interest Centers

	Books/Stories Fingerplay	Music/ Movement	Creative Expression	Small Motor/ Manipulatives	Games/ Large Muscle	Science/Math Cooking	Special Event
Monday							
Tuesday							
Wednesday							
Thursday							
Friday							

© Early Childhood Directors Association (ECDA) 450 North Syndicate, Suite 5, St. Paul, MN 55104

Daily Planning Form

Theme _____ Date _____

Circle Time _____

Learning Centers - Choice Time

    1. _____

    2. _____

    3. _____

    4. _____

    5. _____

    6. _____

Teacher Directed Activities

    A. _____

    B. _____

    C. _____

Special Events_____

_____

Things to do today _____

_____

_____

Notes on children _____

_____

_____

_____

Art Area Procedures

Art is self-expression and art offers a way for children to enjoy learning while having fun. Self-expression should be carried out with freedom in a relaxed atmosphere. Art activities should be an opportunity to explore and experiment with a variety of materials. The process should be the most important part—**not the product**.

Children need encouragement to explore art materials and methods in their own way. Young children should not be forced to copy a model. They may become discouraged and dissatisfied if they do not meet specified standards set by adults.

a. A variety of materials should be available to children at all times for their spontaneous creative experiences. They need to be easily accessible, clearly marked and they need to be replenished.

- crayons
- water color paints
- chalk
- objects for tracing
- markers
- a variety of paper
- scissors

- easel always set up
- clay or playdough
- scraps of colored paper
- paste
- glue
- string
- tape

b. Avoid having more than 4 children doing the same activity; always make several art options available.

c. Children should always be able to move freely from one activity to another.

d. Children need to be responsible for returning materials to their place. The area should be clearly labeled.

e. Children need help in organizing their work area to keep spills and clean up to a minimum. Sponges and water need to be available to children.

f. Adults in the room should not make models for children but encourage children to enjoy making things on their own.

g. Explain expectations and limits of any activity for the group before children begin; define the area available to them.

h. Never ask a child who is working with art materials, "What is it?" They may not know. Rather initiate discussion by saying, "Can you tell me about your work? I like how you used those lines."

i. Art work should be neatly matted on colored construction paper.

© Early Childhood Directors Association (ECDA) 450 North Syndicate, Suite 5, St. Paul, MN 55104

The following list of activity or interest centers encourages and supports self-initiated learning experiences for school-age children. The amount of equipment must be suitable to the ages and skill levels of the children as well as total numbers of children enrolled in a given program.

Activity/Interest Center	Exploration	Examples
Creative Construction	Science, Math and Social Studies Children need opportunities for non-directed, creative activities that fulfill a sense of industry—to be able to make something that can be taken home or used.	Make it, take it construction out of recyclable materials like cardboard tubes, cloth, paper, tape, wire, etc. Wood working, needlecrafts, paper crafts and cooking projects.
Building and Imaginative Play	Children need opportunity to build and manipulate a variety of materials to create environments for imaginative play. Space needs to be provided for uninterrupted construction that can be left for a period of time or from day-to-day.	Building with lego blocks, wooden unit blocks, tinker toy blocks, and a wide variety of props or accessories to make-believe.
Fine Arts	Children need a variety of opportunities to observe and experience the performing arts.	Drama, puppetry, dance, music, graphic arts, easel arts, sculpting, etc.
Individual Hideaway	Because children have been with a group for a major portion of their day, provision for privacy through arranging small, quiet areas that are inviting to children is essential. Children often seek time to be alone to rest, reflect, read, do homework.	Loft, quiet pillow corner, large boxes to create quiet space, study carrels, dividers, etc.
Puzzles	A variety of puzzles can be self-educative tools for trial and error construction.	Puzzle, variety of puzzles, problem solving situations
Table Games	A variety of board and cognitive games help develop: problem solving, strategy setting, peer cooperation and competition, as well as direction following.	Table games, chess, checkers, board games, tournaments
Science, Math, Social Studies and Exploration	Centers should be set up where children can experiment, investigate and explore on a non-threatening, creative, problem solving basis.	Experiments, math and science games, small motors to take apart and investigate, plants, animals, computers, and other electronics

Continued

Activity/Interest Center	Exploration	Examples
Clubs, Organizations, and Other Resources	To further the growth of independence and responsibility in school-age children, children should be encouraged to participate in other supervised activities offered by other youth-serving agencies. Children should be supervised in making a transition between one program and another.	Boy and girl scouts, campfire, 4-H, religious groups, chess club, team sports, intramural sports, music lessons, parks and recreation activities, i.e., cheerleading, magic classes, bowling, drawing, sports, dance, theater groups, etc.
Field Trips	School-age children have a particular interest in exploring the world around them, and local field trips are an effective way of utilizing this interest. Especially on non-school days, children should have the opportunity to explore the broader community that reflects the cultural and economic tone of the community.	Nature centers, parks, zoos, theaters, swimming pools, ice and roller rinks, community centers, humane societies, libraries, science and art museums, historical sites, cultural events, health facilities, bakery, feed mill, farms, newspaper, banks and county parks.
Literature	A space in which it is comfortable and inviting to explore a variety of written material can enhance children's interest and enjoyment of reading as a leisure activity.	Individual browsing, stories read by older children, tapes of stories, trips to libraries, flannelboard stories, writing centers, listening to records, etc.
Dramatic Play, Role Playing	A variety of props set the stage and allow children to "try on" a variety of occupations, roles and experiences of the real world. 7's and 8's are at the peak of interest in dramatic play, make-believe and adventure.	Props can be made available on a routine basis or as a special event, i.e., set up a bakery after a field trip to the bakery or school kitchen. Props to set such areas as: office, fix-it shop, travel bureau, dentist, shoe shop, hat shop, home hospital, plumber, flower shop, etc.
Health, Safety and Taking Care of One's Self	School-age children need to learn independent skills. They are frequently home alone without adult supervision or adult resources.	Basic first aid, fire prevention, safe bike operation, how to care for bikes, how to use telephone effectively, babysitting, nutrition, personal hygiene, caring for yourself. (food preparation)

Continued

Activity/Interest Center	Exploration	Examples
Active Indoor	Children need to have a variety of activities that allow them to move around and "let off steam." If a gym is not available, other space needs to be provided for moderately active games. Children need opportunities to build skills in: interaction with peers and adults, group dynamics, coordination, score keeping and physical fitness.	Low organized games, dodgeball, leapfrog, 4-square, red rover, etc. Resources: athletes, specialists, rope jumper. Clubs: tumbling, bowling, foosball, etc.
Active Outdoor	Children need to have the opportunity to enjoy a variety of leisure time activities out-of-doors. Because of the variety of resources available to different sites, each individual program needs to capitalize on their own individual resources to introduce children to the most accessible activities.	A variety of durable equipment needs to be available for kids to explore: balls, seeds, frisbees, skates, jump ropes, etc.

Quiet Place Log

Date	Child's Name	Reason for Using Quiet Place	Caregiver's Initials	Time In	Time Out	Behavior Plan on File

Separation Log

Date	Child's Name	Staff Person's Name	Time of Incident	Incident Description	Previous Guidance Methods Used	Separation Time End	Separation Time Begin	Parent Notified	Behavior Plan on File

Biting Log

Date	Time	Location	Name of Child Bitten	Name of Child Biting	Facts Leading up to the Bite	How was this Matter Handled/Method of Discipline	Classroom/ Lead Teacher Responsible	Child/ Staff Ratio

Behavior Record

Complete a record for each time the behavior of the child is observed by you, while the child is under your care.

Date _____ Time of day _____

Describe the circumstances during which the behavior developed. _____

_____

Describe the child's response. Be as specific as you can. _____

_____

_____

How long did you allow the child's behavior to continue until the behavior stopped or you took action? Indicate in minutes. _____

_____

If the behavior did not stop spontaneously, what action did you take?_____

_____

_____

Describe the child's response. Again, be as specific as you can. _____

_____

_____

After your intervention, how long was it before the child was able to return to the group? Indicate in minutes.

_____

_____

_____

Separation from the Group Form

Child's name _____ Date _____

Time _____

Behavior of child _____

_____

_____

_____

_____

What less intrusive methods were used _____

_____

_____

_____

_____

Staff's response _____

_____

_____

_____

_____

Signature of parent _____ Date _____

Signature of staff person _____ Date _____

Signature of director _____ Date _____

Place this form in child's folder.

© Early Childhood Directors Association (ECDA) 450 North Syndicate, Suite 5, St. Paul, MN 55104

Persistent Unacceptable Behavior Plan

Child's name _____ Date _____

Behavior of the child _____

_____

_____

_____

_____

Actions taken in the past by the staff _____

_____

_____

_____

_____

Parent comments _____

_____

_____

_____

_____

Agreed upon actions to be taken by the staff to address the behavior _____

_____

_____

_____

_____

Date to be reviewed _____

Signature of parent _____ Date _____

Signature of staff person _____ Date _____

Signature of director _____ Date _____

(Place this form in the child's file)

Conferences

Observations

In this section you will find forms helpful in assessing and recording information about individual children—their development, growth and behavior.

Conferences

In this section you will find forms helpful in scheduling and conducting teacher-parent conferences. There are samples of general conference forms as well as conference forms for various age children (e.g. infant, toddler, preschool).

New Child Observation Report

Child's Name _____

Child's Group _____

Staff Member(s) Completing Report _____

Separation _____
_____
_____

Breakfast _____

Morning Activities _____
_____

Lunch _____

Nap/Quiet Time _____
_____

Early Afternoon Activities _____
_____

Snack _____

Later Afternoon Activities _____
_____

Daily Observation of Individual Child

Child's Name _____ Observers _____

Age _____

Date _____

1. What activities did this child participate in, and with whom? _____

_____

_____

2. What behaviors did you particularly notice? _____

_____

_____

3. What skills were evident? _____

_____

_____

4. Anything else you've noticed in the last few days? _____

_____

_____

5. Based upon what was observed today, what activities and goals might we plan for this child in the future?

_____

_____

6. What could we tell this child's parents about his/her day? What observed information might go into this child's

behavior summary or permanent record? _____

_____

_____

© Early Childhood Directors Association (ECDA) 450 North Syndicate, Suite 5, St. Paul, MN 55104

Daily Observation of Individual Child

Adjustment to School

A. Separation

_____ Confident

_____ Needs teacher help

_____ Fearful

Comments:

B. Routines and Rules

_____ Understands and follows ground rules

_____ Seems to understand but does not always follow ground rules

_____ Is working on gaining an understanding of the ground rules

Comments:

C. Peer Relationships

_____ Seeks out other children

_____ Waits for others to initiate friendship

_____ Solitary play

_____ Parallel play

_____ Cooperative play

_____ Has difficulty cooperating in certain situations

Comments:

Participation in Program

A. Favorite Activities: _____

_____

B. Group Experiences

_____ Usually participates

_____ Needs encouragement with participation

Parent–Teacher Conference Request Form

Date _____

Dear Parent,
We are required by licensing to offer parent-teacher conferences twice a year. This month we are offering conferences.

Please return this to your child's teacher by _____

_____ I would like a conference.

_____ I do not wish to have a conference at this time.

Signed _____

Date _____

Parent–Teacher Conference Request Form

Dear Parents,

I will be having conferences this month between _____ and _____.
You have been scheduled for a conference on _____ at _____.
Please complete and return the portion below the dotted line.
_ _
_____ I can attend on _____ at _____.

_____ I cannot attend at this time and suggest _____

Thank you for your cooperation.

Signed _____

Parent–Teacher Conference Record

Child _____

Conference period _____

Staff Person conducting the conference _____

_____ Parent participated in conference

    Conference date _____

    Name of parent participating _____

_____ Parent did not participate in conference

Parent–Teacher Conference Record

Child's Name _____

Initial Conference (Interview) Date _____

Date of Enrollment _____

At least two conferences must be offered annually. The initial interview will be counted.

Date Offered	Date Held	Time	Remarks	Parent Signature	Staff Signature

Record each conference offering and indicate if not accepted.

Parent Conference Summary Sheet

Child's name _____ Conference date _____

Teacher _____

Parent(s) present _____

General summary of conference _____
_____
_____
_____

Parent concerns or requests_____
_____
_____
_____

Any additional goals set at conference_____
_____
_____
_____

Additional information about child gathered at conference_____
_____
_____
_____

Teacher's plans for follow up to conference_____
_____
_____
_____

Infant Conference Form

Child _____ Birthdate _____

9 - 10 months
1. Localizes sound
2. Can get into sitting position
3. Creeps/crawls
4. Picks up small objects using thumb and forefinger
5. Pulls cover off toy he/she has seen hidden
6. Pulls self up
7. Holds furniture and walks around it
8. Can control lips around cup
9. Imitates sounds
10. Imitates gestures and facial expressions
Comments:

_____

Signature of parent _____ Date _____

11 - 12 months
1. Stands alone
2. Lowers self from standing alone
3. Climbs up and down stairs
4. Walks with one hand held
5. Drinks from cup
6. Is possessive of materials
7. Knows a few words
Comments:

_____

Signature of parent _____ Date _____

13 - 14 months
1. First steps
2. Throws ball
3. Points to familiar body parts
4. Recognizes objects by name
5. Makes lines with pencils/crayons
6. Turns pages of cardboard book
7. Builds a tower with blocks
Comments:

_____

Signature of parent _____ Date _____

15 - 16 months
1. Imitates environmental and animal sounds
2. Feeds self with spoon, but may spill
3. Indicates wants by pointing
4. Kneels without support
5. Brings stool to use for reaching something
6. Names things when pointed to
7. Connects/disconnects large beads
Comments:

_____

Signature of parent _____ Date _____

Child's name _____

Age _____ Date _____

Teachers _____

Gross motor development

1. General coordination:

_____ very awkward _____ somewhat awkward _____ adequate _____ very good

Comments _____

2. General interest in activities:

_____ avoids _____ some interest _____ adequate _____ strong interest

Comments _____

3. Walking:

_____ needs help _____ somewhat awkward _____ adequate _____ very smooth

Comments _____

4. Running:

_____ does not _____ awkward _____ somewhat awkward _____ smooth (adult)

Comments _____

5. Hopping:

_____ cannot _____ 2 or 3 hops _____ hops well

Comments _____

6. Stair climbing:

UP _____ cannot _____ needs help _____ does not alternate _____ alternates
DOWN _____ cannot _____ needs help _____ does not alternate _____ alternates

Comments _____

7. Climbing:

_____ cannot _____ awkward _____ adequate _____ very well

Comments _____

8. Sitting in a chair:

_____ needs help _____ crawls up and turns around _____ adult-like

Comments _____

9. Jumping in place:

_____ awkward _____ 2 or 3 times _____ jumps well

Comments _____

Continued

206 FORMS KIT

10. Jumping from height of one foot:
_____ refuses _____ wants help _____ alone/cautious _____ confident _____ energetic

Comments _____

11. Ball kicking:
_____ cannot _____ awkward _____ kicks well

Comments _____

12. Ball throwing:
_____ cannot _____ wild _____ general direction

Comments _____

13. Trike riding:
_____ cannot _____ only climbs on _____ pushes with feet _____ pedals

Comments _____

Fine motor development

1. General coordination (hand-eye):
_____ very awkward _____ somewhat awkward _____ adequate _____ very good

Comments _____

2. General interest:
_____ avoids _____ some interest _____ strong interest _____ adequate

Comments _____

3. Cutting:
_____ cannot _____ slashes only _____ choppy _____ fairly smooth _____ smooth on line _____ alternates left/
right

Comments _____

4. Drawing grip:
_____ hammer _____ crude opposition _____ adult _____ alternates left/right

Comments _____

5. Drawing control on paper:
_____ off paper _____ only in one area _____ uses whole paper

Comments _____

6. Puzzles:
_____ cannot _____ easily frustrated _____ needs help _____ tries _____ succeeds easily

Comments _____

Continued

7. Picking up objects:
_____ using palms _____ fingertips _____ slides object to edge of table

Comments _____

Perceptual Concepts

1. Body parts (N=name R=recognize)
_____ eye _____ ears _____ nose _____ mouth _____ arm _____ head
_____ fingers _____ leg _____ foot _____ toes _____ elbow _____ wrist
_____ ankle _____ cheek _____ shoulder

Comments _____

2. Sorting:
_____ shapes matched _____ pictures sorted

Comments _____

3. Color (N-name R=recognizes)
_____ red _____ blue _____ purple _____ green _____ orange _____ black
_____ white _____ yellow

Comments _____

Language Development

1. Imitates sounds or words:
_____ does not _____ adequate _____ very well

Comments _____

2. Understanding:
_____ visual response _____ verbal response _____ no response

Comments _____

3. Follows simple directions:
_____ half the time _____ always _____ occasionally

Comments _____

4. Speech:
_____ none _____ a few single words _____ 2 words with meaning _____ 3 word sentences _____ full adult
sentences

Comments _____

5. Intelligibility:
_____ not understandable _____ can make it out _____ easily understood

Comments _____

Continued

6. Names objects and pictures:
_____ not at all _____ a few _____ many

Comments _____

Social and Emotional Development

1. Initiation of activity:
_____ never initiates _____ seldom _____ often

Comments _____

2. Participation in play:
_____ just watches _____ upset when asked _____ eager to participate

Comments _____

3. Attention span:
_____ 30 seconds or less _____ 1 minute _____ 2 minutes _____ longer

Comments _____

4. Interaction with other children (play):
_____ watches _____ plays by self _____ one to one _____ small group
Who does child play with? _____

Comments _____

5. Sharing toys and protection of personal rights:
_____ passive (lets others take toys)
_____ cries, but does not defend rights
_____ physically defends rights
_____ uses words to defend rights

Comments _____

6. Curiosity:
_____ little _____ moderate _____ very curious

Comments _____

7. Frustration tolerance and problem solving: _____

_____

_____

8. Relationship with teacher: _____

_____

_____

© Early Childhood Directors Association (ECDA) 450 North Syndicate, Suite 5, St. Paul, MN 55104

9. Limits and routine: _____

_____

_____

10. Self-concept and general disposition: _____

_____

_____

11. Cooperates in group clean up:
_____ watches _____ refuses when asked _____ reluctant _____ eager

Self Help

1. Eating: _____

_____

2 . Sleeping: _____

_____

3. Toileting: _____

_____

4. Dressing: _____

_____

Goals and Objectives

_____

_____

_____

_____

Parent Signature _____ Date _____

Rating form for 2-year-olds (from age two to age three)

Name of Child _____ Birthdate _____

Starting date _____ Date _____ Teacher's Name _____

LARGE MOTOR DEVELOPMENT

	Almost Never	Occasionally	Frequently	Almost Always
Runs				
Climbs furniture and obstacles				
Walks up steps without help				
Walks backward on command				
Kicks ball successfully				
Throws ball overhand				

SMALL MOTOR DEVELOPMENT

Stacks blocks three high				
Handles scissors for random cutting				
Handles crayons for scribbling				
Unwraps, e.g. candy, bananas				
Takes simple objects apart without difficulty				

LANGUAGE DEVELOPMENT

Uses words to express wants				
Talks—names 10-15 objects and has a small noun/verb vocabulary				
Complies with 1-step directions				
Makes 2-or 3-word sentences				
Uses pronoun me and my				

COGNITIVE DEVELOPMENT

Know he's/she's a boy/girl				
Points to body parts on direction				
Names 3 pictures in picture book				
Counts to 2; aware of 1 more; knows how many to 2				
Understands opposites come - go, push - pull, run - stop				
Matches—compares familiar objects as to color, form or size; groups similar objects				
Listens to singing rhymes				
Recognizes primary colors				

SOCIAL DEVELOPMENT

*KEY: Almost Never - Less than 10% of the time
Occasionally - 25% of the time
Frequently - 75% of the time
Almost Always - At least 90% of the time

Continued

© Early Childhood Directors Association (ECDA) 450 North Syndicate, Suite 5, St. Paul, MN 55104

	Almost Never	Occasionally	Frequently	Almost Always
Shows affection for people, regard for possessions				
Separates from parent easily				
Occupies self on simple suggestion; initiates own activities				
Plays beside with sustained interest				
Accepts limits set by adults				

EMOTIONAL DEVELOPMENT

	Almost Never	Occasionally	Frequently	Almost Always
Explores, investigates surroundings				
Appears relaxed and at ease in preschool setting				
Can wait a short while				
Can tolerate slight frustration				

RESPONSIBILITY AND SELF-HELP SKILLS

	Almost Never	Occasionally	Frequently	Almost Always
Drinks from cup without spills				
Uses spoon/fork successfully				
Partly dresses & undresses self for outdoors				
Helps to pick up				
Washes hands independently				
Urinates in toilet				
Bowel movement in toilet				

*KEY: Almost Never - Less than 10% of the time
Occasionally - 25% of the time
Frequently - 75% of the time
Almost Always - At least 90% of the time

Parent Signature _____ Date _____

Rating form for 3-year-olds (from age three to age four)

Name of Child _____ Birthdate _____

Starting date _____ Date _____

Teacher's Name _____

LARGE MOTOR DEVELOPMENT

	Almost Never	Occasionally	Frequently	Almost Always
Runs smoothly				
Climbs easily				
Jumps with two feet				
Balances briefly				
Walks downstairs (1 step per tread)				
Throws ball purposefully				

SMALL MOTOR DEVELOPMENT

Left ___ Right ___ Switches ___

	Almost Never	Occasionally	Frequently	Almost Always
Accurately cuts lines and shapes with scissors				
Exhibits well-developed hand-eye coordination (e.g. stringing, lacing small manipulative toys)				
Copies circle				
Builds tower				

LANGUAGE DEVELOPMENT

	Almost Never	Occasionally	Frequently	Almost Always
Articulates clearly				
Verbalizes needs				
Understands and follows directions				
Converses (short sentences—simple ideas)				
Uses plurals				

COGNITIVE DEVELOPMENT

	Almost Never	Occasionally	Frequently	Almost Always
Points and counts 1-5				
Compares size (big or little)				
Identifies forms as visually "same" or "different"				
Recognizes first name written in upper and lower case				
Knows first and last name				
Knows colors (red, blue, green, yellow, orange, purple, brown, black, white)				

SOCIAL DEVELOPMENT

*KEY: Almost Never - Less than 10% of the time
Occasionally - 25% of the time
Frequently - 75% of the time
Almost Always - At least 90% of the time

Continued

	Almost Never	Occasionally	Frequently	Almost Always
Plays beside with sustained interest				
Uses language to interact with others				
Approaches other children				
Interacts with other children				
Shares				
Involves self in group activities and routines				
Accepts limits set by adults				
Separates from parent easily				

EMOTIONAL DEVELOPMENT

Approaches new situations calmly and comfortably				
Verbalizes feelings				
Controls aggressive behavior				
Appears relaxed and at ease in the preschool setting				

RESPONSIBILITY AND SELF-HELP SKILLS

Puts on shoes and crosses laces				
Dresses self for outdoors				
Makes own choice of free play activities				
Uses toys appropriately				
Helps to clean up				
Toilet trained				
Uses toilet without help				
Mealtime independence				
Washes hands competently				

*KEY: Almost Never - Less than 10% of the time
Occasionally - 25% of the time
Frequently - 75% of the time
Almost Always - At least 90% of the time

Comments _____

_____

Parent Signature _____ Date _____

Name _____ Teacher _____ Date _____

Social Emotional Readiness
_____ Is self-confident
_____ Shows play initiative
_____ Shares and takes turns
_____ Demonstrates self-control
_____ Refrains from physical aggression
_____ Joins in conversation with teachers _____ classmates _____
_____ Seeks help if needed
_____ Remains with one activity for a length of time
_____ Independently solves group or individual problems
_____ Resists distractions
_____ Demonstrates control over emotions
_____ Is cooperative

Intellectual–Language Readiness
_____ Can express thoughts using sentences _____ speaks clearly _____
_____ Listens attentively in group discussions
_____ Follows directions given to group
_____ Follows directions given to individual
_____ Recognizes: First name _____ Last name _____
        Colors _____ Shapes _____ Numbers 1-10 _____
        Alphabet (non-sequence)
_____ Can write first name
_____ Is able to make choices
_____ Remembers teachers' names

Physical Readiness
_____ Dresses independently
_____ Uses and cares for materials properly
_____ Handles bathroom and snack routines independently
_____ Cleans up when directed
_____ Properly uses scissors, pencil and crayons
_____ Catches a ball
_____ Hops on one foot
_____ Jumps with both feet off the ground
_____ Walks a straight line
_____ Walks backwards

Continued

Areas of Interest

_____ Responds to stories and fingerplays

_____ Responds to music

_____ Enjoys reading books independently

_____ Happily uses markers, paint, playdough and glue

_____ Responds positively to cutting

_____ Enjoys physical activities

_____ Curious about science and nature

_____ Enjoys dramatic and imaginative play

_____ Uses small manipulatives (beads, puzzles, legos, games)

Comments:

Parent Signature _____ Date _____

Staff Signature _____ Date _____

Child's Name _____ Birthdate _____ Age _____

Date _____ Teacher _____

I. Parent Information

A. What are your child's feelings toward the program?

B. Are your expectations for your child being met at the program?

C. What responsibilities does your child have at home?

D. Are there any special situations you would like us to be made aware of?

II. Adjustment to School

Fall   Spring

               A. Separation

_____   _____   Confident

_____   _____   Needs teacher help

_____   _____   Fearful

               B. Routines and Rules

_____   _____   Understands and follows ground rules

_____   _____   Seems to understand but does not follow ground rules

_____   _____   Is working on gaining an understanding of the ground rules

               C. Peer Relationships

_____   _____   Seeks out other children

_____   _____   Waits for others to initiate friendship

_____   _____   Solitary play

_____   _____   Parallel play

_____   _____   Cooperative play

_____   _____   Has difficulty cooperating in certain situations

               D. Relationship with Teachers

_____   _____   Good rapport

_____   _____   Usually works independently of teachers

_____   _____   Is quite dependent upon teachers

               E. Individual Work Habits

_____   _____   Works independently

_____   _____   Needs encouragement to work independently

_____   _____   Needs encouragement finding appropriate work

_____   _____   Good concentration skills

_____   _____   Developing concentration skills

_____   _____   Completes a work cycle

_____   _____   Needs encouragement completing a work cycle

Continued

© Early Childhood Directors Association (ECDA) 450 North Syndicate, Suite 5, St. Paul, MN 55104

F. Clothes and Belongings
_____ _____ Independently cares for belongings
_____ _____ Appropriate help as needed
_____ _____ Needs encouragement
_____ _____ Independently dresses self and zips jacket

III. Participation in Program

A. Group Participation   Favorite Activities
_____ _____ Usually participates
_____ _____ Needs encouragement to participate

B. Language
_____ _____ Speaks clearly
_____ _____ Speaks in sentences
_____ _____ Muscle development

IV. Small Muscle

_____ _____ Holds and uses crayon/pencil correctly
_____ _____ Holds and uses scissors correctly
_____ _____ Traces a line accurately
_____ _____ Cuts on a straight line
_____ _____ Cuts a circle
_____ _____ Explores variety of art materials

V. Large Muscle

_____ _____ Hops or jumps
_____ _____ Walks forward on a balance beam
_____ _____ Walks backwards on a balance beam
_____ _____ Manipulates self on climber
_____ _____ Enjoys outdoor play
_____ _____ Runs with control (stop, change direction, etc.)

VI. Cognitive Development

A. Visual Perception
_____ _____ Matches basic shapes and sizes
_____ _____ Names basic colors
_____ _____ Recognizes like objects
_____ _____ Recognizes printed name

B. Mathematics
_____ _____ Names the basic shapes
_____ _____ Counts by rote 1 to _____
_____ _____ Counts objects 1 to 20

Comments:

Fall Conference Date _____ Parent Signature _____

Spring Conference Date _____ Parent Signature _____

© Early Childhood Directors Association (ECDA) 450 North Syndicate, Suite 5, St. Paul, MN 55104

Conference Form for Preschool

Name _____ Class _____ Date _____

Teacher _____ Aide _____

The continuum indicated at the right is a means of recording the child's participation as observed by the teacher.

	Is Learning	Usually	Always	Not Applicable
Self Help Skills				
Solves problems without adult help	_____	_____	_____	_____
Social Emotional				
Shows self control	_____	_____	_____	_____
Displays constructive self motivation	_____	_____	_____	_____
Follows class routines/directions	_____	_____	_____	_____
Participates in group activities	_____	_____	_____	_____
Attentive during group times	_____	_____	_____	_____
Stays on task	_____	_____	_____	_____
Respects and interacts with peers	_____	_____	_____	_____
Play				
Individual	_____	_____	_____	_____
Side by side (parallel)	_____	_____	_____	_____
With 1 or 2 friends (cooperative)	_____	_____	_____	_____
With group	_____	_____	_____	_____
Initiates play	_____	_____	_____	_____
Use of Material (Free Play)				
Art	_____	_____	_____	_____
Books/records	_____	_____	_____	_____
Cognitive activities	_____	_____	_____	_____
Dramatic Play	_____	_____	_____	_____
Manipulatives(cars, puzzles, etc.)	_____	_____	_____	_____
Science	_____	_____	_____	_____
Sensory (sand table, water table, wood working bench)	_____	_____	_____	_____
Participates in clean up time	_____	_____	_____	_____
Other _____	_____	_____	_____	_____
Physical Development				
Participates in small muscle skill development	_____	_____	_____	_____
Participates in large muscle skill development	_____	_____	_____	_____

Teacher Comments:

Parent Signature _____ Date _____

Date _____

For Period _____ to _____

Social/Emotional Development

What is his/her disposition and usual facial expression and appearance? _____
_____

How does the child respond and react to the teacher? Is he/she antagonistic, dependent, independent, subservient, cooperative, attention-seeking, friendly, negative, timid? _____
_____

How does the child respond and react to the parent? _____
_____

Your child indicated the following possible personality traits:_____
_____

A. During times of frustration or tension:

Hits	Throws tantrums	Wants adult assurance
Kicks	Yells	Understands situation and adjusts
Bites	Cries	Sucks thumb or finger
Scratches	Increased state of activity	
Spits	Pulls hair	Withdrawn
Pinches	Appropriate verbal expression	

Comments _____

8. With the group your child is:

Leader	Boisterous	Uncooperative	Quarrelsome
Follower	Reticent	Determined	Good loser
Shy	Cooperative	Timid	Poor loser
Accepted	Content	Creative	Funny

Comments _____

Your child needs improvement in:

Use of language	Sharing possessions and equipment
Enjoying other children	Accepting failure and frustrations
Accepting new people	Overcoming fears
Self-entertainment	Learning to relax
Greater self-confidence	Greater attention span
Accepting limits	Learning to take turns
Independence	Cooperating with adults
	Cooperating with children

Continued

Play Patterns

What activities repeatedly interest the child?

Your child enjoys

Legos	Stories	Clapping hands	Climbing
Blocks	Cutting	Puzzles	Bikes
Easel painting	Clay	Finger paint	Swings
Pasting	Doll corner	Water play	Sand
Crayons	Books	Walks	Sledding
Games	Singing	Rhythm band	Trucks & Cars

Other _____

Intellectual Development

Alertness to environment; his type of interest, use of judgment, language development, vocabulary, and its improvement. Attention span at various activities, special skills; follows directions

Physical Development

Describe the child's appearance, general health, disabilities, energy, coordination, large and small muscle, skill in use of equipment, e.g. scissors, pencils, climbers, bikes, manipulatives

Routines

Reaction upon arrival _____
Putting away toys and helping with clean-up _____

Independence in dressing, tying shoes etc. _____

Toileting, washing _____

Sleeping habits _____

Eating habits _____

General Comments   Parent's Response to Conference

_____	_____
_____	_____
_____	_____
_____	_____

Name _____ Birthday _____ Age _____

Date_____

Teachers _____

LARGE MUSCLE DEVELOPMENT: locomotor movement and coordination. Activities include: running, jumping, climbing, exercises, balancing, and games.

1st Year		2nd Year		
SPR	FALL	SPR	FALL	
___	___	___	___	Enjoys indoor activities
___	___	___	___	Enjoys outdoor activities
___	___	___	___	Is developing well for age
___	___	___	___	Movement patterns are sometimes unbalanced and out of control
___	___	___	___	Movement patterns are consistently unbalanced and out of control
___	___	___	___	Needs encouragement
___	___	___	___	Sometimes over-eager and loses control
___	___	___	___	Cautious

FINE MOTOR DEVELOPMENT: Skill in handling manipulative materials. Activities include: cutting, pasting, painting, coloring puzzles, stringing, peg work and transference.

___	___	___	___	Is developing well for age
___	___	___	___	Confident
___	___	___	___	Needs assistance and practice
___	___	___	___	Tense
___	___	___	___	Uncertain

ORGANIZED GROUP EXPERIENCE: Stories, games, group time music, finger plays and sharing.

___	___	___	___	Pays attention
___	___	___	___	Contributes relevant ideas and information
___	___	___	___	Participates in a variety of group activities
___	___	___	___	Needs reminders
___	___	___	___	Distracting to group
___	___	___	___	Indifferent
___	___	___	___	Hesitant
___	___	___	___	Often interrupts

WORK HABITS: Establishing a foundation of order, a good cycle of activity, concentration skills and self confidence for successful learning.

___	___	___	___	Shows self-initiative
___	___	___	___	Confident
___	___	___	___	Proudly shares personal accomplishments
___	___	___	___	Seeks help often
___	___	___	___	Reluctant to try
___	___	___	___	Easily frustrated
___	___	___	___	Needs encouragement to choose materials
___	___	___	___	Is easily distracted
___	___	___	___	Chooses to work alone

___	___	___	___	Completes a work cycle
___	___	___	___	Detached and dreamy
___	___	___	___	Difficulty following directions
___	___	___	___	Follows directions

RESPECT FOR THE ENVIRONMENT:

___	___	___	___	Shows care in the use of materials
___	___	___	___	Is careless with materials
___	___	___	___	Cooperates in room clean up
___	___	___	___	Frequently needs reminders to clean up

COMMUNICATION: Listening and speaking skills.

___	___	___	___	Usually listens attentively
___	___	___	___	Sometimes has difficulty listening
___	___	___	___	Clearly expresses self verbally
___	___	___	___	Difficulty being understood

SOCIAL AND EMOTIONAL DEVELOPMENT: A child's sense of responsibility for themselves, their friends and experiences.

Self-Esteem

___	___	___	___	Seems to have a good self-esteem
___	___	___	___	Seems to sometimes lack self confidence

Handling of emotional situations

___	___	___	___	Expresses feeling in appropriate manner
___	___	___	___	Attempts to settle minor conflicts independently
___	___	___	___	Cries easily
___	___	___	___	Easily frustrated
___	___	___	___	Extremely sensitive
___	___	___	___	Acts silly
___	___	___	___	Responds physically
___	___	___	___	Withdraws

Relationship with children

___	___	___	___	Shows thoughtfulness and sensitivity
___	___	___	___	Likes a variety of children
___	___	___	___	Has special friends
___	___	___	___	Difficulty respecting other children's rights

Relationship with adults

___	___	___	___	Has a good rapport with adults
___	___	___	___	Seeks adult help when needed
___	___	___	___	Is often dependent upon adults
___	___	___	___	Follows through reluctantly with adult direction

Continued

COGNITIVE SKILLS: Pre-reading, reading, sensorial and math

—— —— —— —— Knows colors: red yellow blue green orange black white
gray brown pink purple
—— —— —— —— Knows shapes: circle triangle square rectangle
—— —— —— —— Advanced shapes: (list) _____
—— —— —— —— Understands concept of matching
—— —— —— —— Classification
—— —— —— —— Sequencing
—— —— —— —— Rote Counting: 0 1 2 3 4 5 6 7 8 9 10 11 12 13 14 15 16 17 18 19 20
—— —— —— —— Quantity Counting: 0 1 2 3 4 5 6 7 8 9 10 11 12 13 14 15 16 17 18 19 20
—— —— —— —— Number recognition: 0 1 2 3 4 5 6 7 8 9 10 11 12 13 14 15 16 17 18 19 20
—— —— —— —— Alphabet Recognition: Lower case
a b c d e f g h i j k l m n o p q r s t u v w x y z
—— —— —— —— Phonics: Knows sounds the letter makes.
1) m t p a n 2) s d g h i 3) b r f c u 4) j k l o y 5) z v q w x e
—— —— —— —— Printing: Lower case
a b c d e f g h i j k l m n o p q r s t u v w x y z
—— —— —— —— Prints name: Upper case _____ Lower case _____
—— —— —— —— Word construction
—— —— —— —— Reading

SELF-HELP SKILLS:

—— —— —— —— Feels confident and comfortable dressing
—— —— —— —— Needs help with dressing skills
—— —— —— —— Needs reminders and encouragement
—— —— —— —— Resists dressing routine
—— —— —— —— Needs some assistance in toileting

FAVORITE ACTIVITIES:

——	——	——	——	Puzzles	——	——	——	——	Transference
——	——	——	——	Books	——	——	——	——	Housekeeping
——	——	——	——	Blocks	——	——	——	——	Construction
——	——	——	——	Music	——	——	——	——	Shelf materials
——	——	——	——	Projects	——	——	——	——	Manipulatives
——	——	——	——	Large Muscle	——	——	——	——	Dramatic Play

Teacher's Comments _____

Parent's Comments _____

Parent Signature _____ Date _____

Health and Safety

This section includes forms to assist you in maintaining safe and healthy environment for the children and staff in your program. Examples of forms included in this section are accident log, immunization record log, communicable disease notification form, checklist for health and safety conditions and hazards inspection record.

Accident Log

Mark Date and Time Where Applicable

Child's Name	Child's Age	Date of Accident	Time of Accident	How and Where Accident Occurred	Type of Injury	Parent Notified	MD Notified	Child Released/Parent	Child Released/EMT	Child Kept at Center	Treatment	Initials

Illness Report Log

Program _____

Child's Name and Age	Date Reported	Date of Onset of Symptoms	Symptoms	Date of Absence or Exclusion	Date Returned to Center (if Applicable)	Diagnosis	Medications	Seen by MD	Staff Name

Immunization Record Log

Child's Name	Date of Physical	DPT #1	#2	#3	#4	Polio #1	#2	#3	#4	Boosters MMR	TBN	Other	Comments

Daily Food Temperatures Log

(Food Prepared at Center)

Center _____   Month _____

Date/Time	Main Course	Temperature	Initials

Hot foods cooked to a temperature of 150° or higher

Leftovers cooked to a temperature of 165° or higher

Cold foods should be 40° or less

Food Allergies and Special Diets Log

Child's Name _____

Foods that are not to be served in any quantity	Foods that can be served in small amounts	Familiar foods that contain the basic food not to be served

Is the child now being, or has the child ever been, treated by a physician for an allergy? When and for how long?

What reactions does the child have when these foods are eaten?

Date _____ Parents signature _____

Tornado Drill Log

Month	Date	Time	# Children/Adults	Evacuation Time	Alternate Exit	Problems

Fire Drill Log

Month	Date	Time	# Children/Adults	Evacuation Time	Alternate Exit	Problems

Date of Incident: Suspected _____ Physical Abuse _____ Sexual Abuse _____ Neglect _____ Other

Reported by _____ Agency _____ Date_____

Address _____ Telephone _____

Relationship to Family _____

Nature of the problem (Including victim's names, injuries, and location where incident occurred):

_____
(continue on back side)

Where is the child(ren) now _____Do parents know about complaint? _____ No _____ Yes

Who else did you contact _____

Others with information _____

Family Information	Mother (DOB) _____	Father (DOB) _____
Name	_____	_____
Address	_____	_____
City & Home phone	_____	_____
Place of employment	_____	_____
Work phone	_____	_____
Other names known by	_____	_____
Previous spouses	_____	_____

Full Names of Children:

Name _____ DOB _____ School _____ Grade _____
Name _____ DOB _____ School _____ Grade _____
Name _____ DOB _____ School _____ Grade _____
Name _____ DOB _____ School _____ Grade _____

Phoned Report To _____ Date _____

Send to _____

Continued

Please draw in location of physical injuries, if applicable

Communicable Disease Notification Form

Date _____, 19 _____

Your child has been exposed to _____ on or about this date

_____. If you would like more information regarding this, please contact

the _____ office.

Thank you

Monthly Health Consultation

Date _____

Brief description of visit _____

_____

_____

Signed: RN _____

Director _____

Health Care Referral

Date _____

Dear Parent:

In our daily health observation of _____ we have noted _____

_____ and we recommend your child be seen by a physician for further

evaluation. Please return the form below so that we may know if special attention is needed. Thank you.

To: Physician

We have referred _____ for further evaluation of _____

_____.

Please indicate below if special attention or observation is needed during child care activities.

Thank you.

Findings _____

Date _____ Signature _____

Health Care Reminder

Date _____

Dear _____

We have been reviewing the health records of the children attending the center. It is required that all children attending a child care program must have current immunizations.

In reviewing _____ health record, we have found the following:
(child s name)

1. _____   No current physical examination form on file,
                enclosed is a physical examination form.

2. _____   Needs additional DPT
                (diphtheria-pertussis-tetanus)

3. _____   Needs additional OPV
                (oral polio vaccine)

4. _____   Needs MMR (measles-mumps-rubella vaccine)

5. _____   Needs a TBN (tuberculin test)

6. _____   Needs HIB (haemophilus influenzae b)

7. _____   Other:

These immunizations may have been given by your physician to your child. Since we do not have a record of the immunization or physical, please have your physician, physician's nurse or immunization clinic nurse complete the health form.

Please return the form(s) by _____
                              Date

Thank you for your cooperation.

Staff _____

© Early Childhood Directors Association (ECDA) 450 North Syndicate, Suite 5, St. Paul, MN 55104

Name _____ Birthdate _____ Classroom _____

Date of injury _____ Time _____ Where did injury occur?

_____

Description of injury _____

Description of incident: How did injury occur? What was the child doing, level of supervision, approximate number of children in area? Specify any equipment involved. _____

_____

_____

Describe any first aid measures given: _____

_____

Who performed the first aid? _____

Persons notified:

      Program administrator _____

      Parents _____ by note? _____ by phone?

      Physician/clinic _____

      Hospital _____

If the injured child received medical care, describe the treatment which was administered.

_____

What are the follow-up instructions? _____

Action taken:

Sent home: Called 911?   Sent to hospital?

_____ yes   _____ no   _____ yes _____ no   _____ yes _____ no

Continued

238 FORMS KIT

Sent to hospital:

_____ Yes _____ No Name of hospital _____

Transported by _____

Doctor's name _____

Witnesses: _____

Adult(s) present when incident occurred:

Name _____ Position _____

Additional witnesses _____

Follow up

What measures could be taken to prevent a similar accident? _____
_____

Staff signature _____ Date _____
Program Administrator signature _____ Date _____

Draw a diagram of the room or area in which the accident/incident occurred. Place an X at the spot of the accident and an S at the places where staff were (one S for each staff person).

© Early Childhood Directors Association (ECDA) 450 North Syndicate, Suite 5, St. Paul, MN 55104

Injury Report Follow-Up Form

Additional Communications with Parents

Date _____

Time _____

By Whom _____

With Whom _____

Content _____

_____

Date _____

Time _____

By whom _____

With whom _____

Content _____

_____

Date _____

Time _____

By whom _____

With whom _____

Content _____

_____

Instructions:

This report is to be filled out for each accident/head bump a child receives at the program.

The Parent's Copy is to be given to the parent when the child is picked up. The parent must sign at the bottom of the Parent's and file copy before the child leaves.

Completed file copies should be filed in _____.

© Early Childhood Directors Association (ECDA) 450 North Syndicate, Suite 5, St. Paul, MN 55104

A. Illness and Infection

1. In the past year, how many staff have been exposed to and/or contacted: _____ head lice _____ flu

   _____ colds _____ sore throat _____ impetigo _____ childhood illness _____ hepatitis _____ giardiasis

2. In the past year, how many staff have worked when sick? _____

3. Is there an adequate and effective substitute policy?_____

4. Is there an established policy for caring for sick children? _____

   Is it always implemented/enforced? _____

5. Is there a separate area set aside for sick children? _____

6. How and where are children diapered? _____

7. How is the diapering area cleaned? _____

   Is this adequate?_____

8. Are staff members screened for rubella? _____ T.B.? _____

B. Body Strains

1. In the past year, how many staff have suffered from back/neck/shoulder or leg strains? _____

2. Is there adult-sized furniture available for staff? _____

3. How often do staff members move heavy equipment or furniture? _____

4. Is there adequate and easily accessible storage available? _____

C. Chemicals and Art Materials

1. Name the chemical cleaners used on-site _____

_____

2. Are all chemicals/cleaners labeled properly with directions for use?_____

3. Do you use: _____ powdered tempera _____ permanent markers _____ dry clay _____ lead glazes

   _____ instant paper mache _____ others _____

4. Have staff members experienced skin, nose, eye, or respiratory problems from cleaning solutions and/or art

   materials?_____

5. Do you spray with pesticides to control fleas, roaches, or other vermin?_____

Continued

D. Stress

1. How many staff members feel their job is stressful? _____

2. What areas do you think are most stressful? _____

3. I have experienced:

_____ headaches _____ trouble sleeping _____ muscle strain _____ eye strain

_____ changes in menstrual cycle _____ digestive/stomach problems _____ nausea/dizziness/exhaustion

How many other staff have experienced:

_____ headaches/trouble sleeping _____ muscle strain _____ eye strain _____ changes in menstrual cycle

_____ digestive/stomach problems _____ nausea/dizziness/exhaustion

4. Are there established, effective policies for: _____ breaks _____ pregnant workers _____ grievance resolution

Hazard Inspection Record

Location	Date	Date
UPSTAIRS CLASSROOM		
Smoke Alarm	_____	_____
Broken Equipment	_____	_____
Dangerous Substances	_____	_____
General Appearance	_____	_____
DOWNSTAIRS CLASSROOM		
Smoke Alarm	_____	_____
Broken Equipment	_____	_____
Dangerous Substances	_____	_____
General Appearance	_____	_____
SMALL DOWNSTAIRS CLASSROOM		
Smoke Alarm	_____	_____
Broken Equipment	_____	_____
Dangerous Substances	_____	_____
General Appearance	_____	_____
HALLWAYS		
Smoke Alarms	_____	_____
Broken Equipment	_____	_____
Exit Lights	_____	_____
General Appearance	_____	_____
BATHROOM		
Broken Equipment	_____	_____
Exit Lights	_____	_____
BIG ROOM		
Smoke Alarms	_____	_____
Broken Equipment	_____	_____
Outlets	_____	_____
General Appearance	_____	_____
BACK ROOM		
Broken Equipment	_____	_____
General Appearance	_____	_____
KITCHEN		
Medicine Chest	_____	_____
Broken Equipment	_____	_____
Flashlight	_____	_____
General Appearance	_____	_____
Dangerous Substances	_____	_____
OFFICE		
Smoke Alarm	_____	_____
Radio	_____	_____
Flashlight	_____	_____
General Appearance	_____	_____
Dangerous Substances	_____	_____
First Aid Box	_____	_____
BACKYARD		
Broken Equipment	_____	_____
Weeds/Dangerous Plants	_____	_____

Daily Hazards Checklist

Room 1
_____ Clean floor
_____ Plugs plugged
_____ Tables in good repair
_____ Chairs in good repair
_____ Trash emptied
_____ Dirty dishes cleaned
_____ Dangerous substances secured
_____ General appearance

Room 2
_____ Clean floor
_____ Plugs plugged
_____ Equipment is safe, put together tight, strong so
no weak points, no broken edges
_____ Carpet is tacked down
_____ Trash emptied
_____ Dirty dishes cleaned
_____ General appearance

Room 3
_____ Clean floor
_____ Plugs plugged
_____ Tables in good repair
_____ Chairs in good repair
_____ Trash emptied
_____ Dirty dishes cleaned
_____ General appearance

Room 4
_____ Clean floor
_____ Plugs plugged
_____ Tables in good repair
_____ Chairs in good repair
_____ Trash emptied
_____ Dirty dishes cleaned
_____ General appearance

Room 5
_____ Clean floor
_____ Plugs plugged
_____ Tables in good repair
_____ Chairs in good repair
_____ Trash emptied
_____ Dangerous substances secured
_____ General appearance

General comments (include dates):_____
_____
_____

Room 6
_____ Clean floor
_____ Plugs plugged
_____ Tables in good repair
_____ Chairs in good repair
_____ Trash emptied
_____ Dirty dishes cleaned
_____ General appearance

Room 7
_____ Clean floor
_____ Plugs plugged
_____ Tables in good repair
_____ Chairs in good repair
_____ Trash emptied
_____ General appearance

Office
_____ Clean floor
_____ First aid boxes intact
_____ Medicine chest
_____ Dangerous substances secured
_____ Trash emptied
_____ General appearance

Boys Bathroom
_____ Clean floor
_____ Soap in dispenser
_____ Paper towels
_____ Toilet paper
_____ Toilets disinfected
_____ Sinks disinfected
_____ Trash emptied
_____ General appearance

Girls Bathroom
_____ Clean floor
_____ Soap in dispenser
_____ Paper towels
_____ Toilet paper
_____ Toilets disinfected
_____ Sinks disinfected
_____ Trash emptied
_____ General appearance

Kitchen
_____ Fire extinguisher
_____ Equipment in good repair
_____ Dangerous substances secured
_____ General appearance

Cleaning Record / Infant Room

Week _____ of _____ to _____

Weekly

_____ Dust blinds/vents

_____ Collect all used sheets (not rubber) and put on clean ones (for those cribs not changed at other times during the week)

_____ Sanitize cribs - large crib room (for those not sanitized at other times during the week)

_____ Sanitize cribs - small crib room (for those not sanitized at other times during the week)

_____ Wipe out and sanitize the ledges in the refrigerator

_____ Clean and sanitize microwave

_____ Sanitize entire changing table

_____ Clean sink area in changing room

_____ Clean and sanitize wooden infant seats

Monthly

_____ Sanitize baseboards (week 1)

_____ Wash all blankets in cribs (week 2)

_____ Dust shelves and organize diapers in changing room on infant side (week 3)

_____ Generally organize top of cubbies, changing table supplies, counter top and cupboards (week 4)

_____ Organize and dispose of "over the counter" medications - white tub (week 4)

Document extra cleaning done (date and initial)

Date	Initial	Specifics
_____	_____	_____
_____	_____	_____
_____	_____	_____
_____	_____	_____
_____	_____	_____

We hope that you have found the forms in this publication appropriate for your early childhood program. We encourage you to use this book as well as other ECDA publications to assist you with your administrative needs.

The following are other ECDA publications that can be ordered:

SURVIVAL KIT FOR EARLY CHILDHOOD DIRECTORS

S O S KIT FOR DIRECTORS

CHILDREN'S KEEPSAKE CALENDAR (undated and multicultural)

POLICIES AND PROCEDURES FOR EARLY CHILDHOOD DIRECTORS

ECDA is also a distributor for **THE EARLY CHILDHOOD SUPER DIRECTOR: MANAGING FOR SUCCESS AND SANITY** written by Sue Baldwin, the ECDA Executive Director.

For further information about any of the above publications, or to receive a membership brochure, you may contact us at:

E.C.D.A.
450 North Syndicate Suite 5
St. Paul, MN. 55104
612-645-6643